A Man of Gold AND Other Stories

Other Books by Ramesh K. Srivastava

Critical Studies

- *Determinism in Hemingway*, 1975
- *Hemingway and His For Whom the Bell Tolls*, 1980
- *Perspectives on Bhabani Bhattacharya* (Editor), 1982
- Thoreau's *Walden* (Editor), 1983
- *Perspectives on Anita Desai* (Editor), 1984
- *Six Indian Novelists in English*, 1987
- *Colonial Consciousness in Black American, African and Indian Fiction in English* (Editor), 1991
- *Critical Studies in English and American Literature*, 1993
- *Symbolism in Indian Fiction in English* (Editor), 1997
- *The Novels of Kamala Markandaya: A Critical Study*, 1998
- *Ten Indian English Writers,* 2005
- *Wit and Humour in Indian English Literature* (Editor), 2008

Creative Writing

- *Love and Animality: Stories*, 1984
- *Cooperative Colony: Stories*, 1985
- *Masks and Men: Stories*, 1986
- *Neema* (a novel), 1986
- *Games They Play and Other Stories*, 1989
- *Under the Lamp: Stories*, 1993
- *Coils of the Serpent* (a novel), 2011
- *Read, Write and Teach: Essays on Learning to Live Together,* 2014
- *Christmas Gift and Other Stories*, 2015
- *My Father's Bad Boy: An Autobiography,* 2017
- *Road Not Taken and Other Stories,* 2018

A Man of Gold AND Other Stories

Ramesh K. Srivastava

AUTHORSPRESS

Worldwide Circulation through Authorspress Global Network
First Published in 2022
by
Authorspress
Q-2A Hauz Khas Enclave, New Delhi-110 016 (India)
Phone: (0) 9818049852
E-mail: authorspressgroup@gmail.com
Website: www.authorspressbooks.com

A Man of Gold and Other Stories
ISBN 978-93-90891-23-8

Printed in India at Thomson Press (India) Limited

To

Two Great People
who shaped and saved my academic career

Dr. Ayodhya Prasad Srivastava
(1-2-1931–24-1-2021)
Professor and Head, Department of Physics
Dr Hari Singh Vishwavidyalaya, Sagar (M.P.)

&

Mrs. Laxmi Kanta Chawla
Ex-Minister of Education, Govt of Punjab &
Former Associate Professor, Hindi Department
B.B.K. D.A.V. College for Women,
Amritsar (Punjab)

ACKNOWLEDGEMENTS

Acknowledgement is gratefully made for permission to reprint the copyrighted material to: *Writers Editors Critics: An International Biannual Refereed Journal of English Language and Literature* for "Perils of Simplicity," "A Memorable Present,"" The Bicycle," "Disposable Items," "Of Far and Near," "A Great Prize," "Resversal" and "The Holy Cow"; to *International Journal of Multicultural Literature* for "The Beauty and the Beast," "Sweet Revelaions," "Two Faces," "Expiation," "The Reconciliator," "A Man of Gold" and "Amnesia"; to K.V. Dominic for "Different from Others;" to *Indian Journal of English Studies* for "A Teacher of Humanity" and "Corridor Therapy;" and to *Contemporary Vibes* for "Sowing Seeds" and "Blessed be the Dark."

Ramesh K. Srivastava

PREFACE

A short story is an artistic portrayal of ever-unfolding mysteries of human existence. It is a tiny mirror that intensely reflects a focused fragment of vast moving kaleidoscope of life that each day, each moment passes by us in its new yet recognisable ever-changing patterns and combinations. It is a frozen moment of life, carrying in it the seeds of perennial truths. It reveals in a flash an image of hitherto unexplored aspect of life fleeing each moment before us. A good short story is like a supply of fresh air that makes the human life delightful, meaningful and no less healthy. It is not, as is occasionally made out to be, an artistic conglomeration of unusual characters, unfamiliar landscapes and witty dialogues to titillate and tickle one's fancy but a literary creation that shows to the reader a patch of greenery here or a bunch of flowers there which to the accustomed eyes had been a piece of uninviting desert land. It must also not be taken merely as a means of entertainment, a traveling companion or a puzzling literary experiment in which a moment is disproportionately stretched and each word of which sends the reader's brain reeling to history, geography and mythology of distant lands.

Whereas the short story would lose its place in serious literature if fashioned solely as a means of modern entertainment, it would also jeopardise its coveted popularity when made out as a complicated and puzzling literary creation. A highly complex and unintelligible story may tease and please an intelligent reader by his sense of discovering something not easily decipherable but confuses an average reader who, suffering from the feeling of belonging to a lower class, grudgingly shares the royal feast albeit not with the same ease and carefreeness with which the high-perched Brahmins would do. Hence unconsciously or consciously, the writer is and must be influenced and his stories molded by the type of readers available for him. To wholly disregard them while carving and whittling a literary piece would be as inappropriate as to play the Western classical music to rickshaw-wallahs.

A fine short story is the joint-product of the heart and the head. It originates from an inspiring idea, an appealing incident, a dramatic-situation, a memorable character or an unforgettable experience. The seed of the story sprouts in the writer's head. It grows and swells to take the shape of a story carrying around it a mass of herbage, like a foetus in amniotic fluid, which protects as well as stunts, and which has to be cleared before its unfurled leaves and its extending branches could assert its separate entity. The fully-grown, well-trimmed plant of the story then stands majestically before the world, concealing the hand that had given it a loving care or oblivious of the seed that had given rise to the creation.

In their earliest forms, the Indian tales date back to the interpolated stories in the *Ramayana* and the *Mahabharata*, the fables in *Panchatantra*, the tales of *Betal*, and the myths and legends abounding in the *Puranas*, as also in ancient Indian literatures of various languages. These too embody enriched moments of life even if paraded in outlandish garbs. They contain the essence of life. The short prose narrative in its present form was pioneered and popularised by the Americans. The basic difference between the short stories as they existed in the past and those we have today is both in their execution and in the intention of their creator. The main thrust of the earliest stories, both Indian and European, was usually religious, moral and reformative but rarely literary. In the modern times, the short stories, some of which could be myths and legends rewritten, have some literary value even if with the undercurrents of moralistic and reformative concerns.

With the shrinking boundaries of the world and with the increasing complexity of modern times, the nature of the short story has also changed considerably. It is no longer a tale relating to the exploits and adventures of gods and goddesses, fairies and witches, kings and queens, and birds and animals told by a grandmother to lull her children to sleep or to sweeten the bitterness of life; instead, it is a powerful and effective means of portraying prismatic reality of our time. Seen from different angles, the short story assumes varied forms, evolving out of different viewpoints, structures and narrative techniques.

Whatever the type of the story, a prerequisite to its being appreciated is that it must be readable. With this end in view, the story must be short, interesting and in a tone that creates a harmonious relationship between the writer and the reader. An appetite, like the one needed to enjoy a hearty meal, has to be created in the reader to see something new in what appears to be the oft-trodden ground, and then to sustain it with legitimate artistic means, such as suspense, humor and irony. An element of wonder originating from such a discovery or from the change of fortunes associated with fairy tales can also have a similar function.

A short story, for Poe, is a classic in miniature with precision-made parts and singleness of effect, the latter being above everything else in the world to which every character, incident, sentence and every word must contribute. The singleness of effect depends largely on the end of the story which, like that of a play, must have a resolution or a sting so as to leave an unambiguous impact on the reader.

The length of the short story is to be determined not by the number of pages or by the duration in which it is read but by its capacity to hold the reader's interest. To talk of the length of the story in terms of pages is to talk of a certain number of people who might make a good company. At times an interesting story read in a desolate place can give the reader better company than would so a bunch of gloomy-faced people in a crowded railway compartment. The story should not be too long to permit unavoidable interruptions and to encroach upon the areas of the novella or the novel. It would have a full impact only if it is short enough to be viewed in totality like the painting of an entire human figure rather than a microscopic scrutiny of his face, his torso or his legs at different times. Indeed, a good impact is like a powerful slap with all fingers and palm striking together which would not be so were they to strike separately. The questions of impact and of length become more relevant for short stories meant for popular magazines, usually devoured by the traveling or relaxing people who invariably prefer short and interesting ones. The story too brief, on the other hand, may have the effect of a cracker's explosion that unnerves one for a moment and then is forgotten. In fact each organic part of the story, as of a human being, is beautiful not in itself but in relation with others. All parts must be so closely woven that nothing can bc added, nothing taken away. Hence the story, like a good sculpture, is not a lifeless assemblage but a receptacle of the artist's vision and soul.

The greatness of the short story writer consists not in creating a memorable menagerie but in painting a realistic picture of life. In order to draw the image of a person, reconstruct an episode, create a scene of terror, highlight the irony of a situation or to paint a personified passion, a writer must select appropriate tools. A beggar in the street is a despicable thing one avoids but a beggar in the story can be a memorable pathetic character, melting all the resistance of the reader till softer feelings gush forth from us. Of course, there are no rules to suggest how all this is to be done perfectly; which characters and incidents to choose and which to reject; what to write and how much to be left to the reader's imagination. Such questions are better left to the artist.

The question of probability and improbability in a fictional work remains a matter of serious concern for critics who would like every word or action to be tested on a Richter scale of their imagination, disregarding the fact that a writer does not buy his material sifted and cleansed of improbable elements from some laboratory but selects it in its crude form directly or vicariously from the life itself. Some elements of improbability liable to be found in such material should not cause undue alarm. One has to pick up any standard newspaper to see that quite a few incidents reported in it are far from probable; for an incident or a character becomes worthy of being reported only when, by being unusual, it touches the fringes of improbability. What one has to avoid are impossibilities – occurrences of unnatural feats and miracles. To superimpose divine exploits on mortals is to encroach in the area of fantasy and fairyland which might be a staple diet for Indian movies and television serials but must be kept out of the short story.

As incidents ought to be probable, characters must be from real life. Some characters are so inimitable that they haunt the memory long after the short story is over. To me the characters many times come with the same intensity as do incidents and situations. Once a character comes before my eyes, small things altogether unconnected crowd my imagination and gravitate meaningfully to the aid of its portrayal. Little by little, a character is formed or transformed till he becomes a perfect presentable creature. I have often looked around in astonishment how diversified the world really is without having two people exactly alike in personality or mental make-up. It has too some beings with the human part missing who, like Shantanu's six sons, would better have been drowned into the Ganges without causing any loss to the society. A couple of such wicked people have troubled me personally for a long time, tried to disturb my tranquility and block the flow of my pen, but I have persevered. Some mysterious power urges me to go on. A folk saying heard in my childhood remains meaningfully embedded in my memory: the dogs bark but the elephant goes on.

Creative imagination does not trudge along a predetermined track, nor can it be shackled by administrative controls. The short story writer is a man of imagination, of moods, and is the sole arbiter of when to write and on what. No subject matter can restrict the writer's vision. He writes of people largely from personal experience, not from mere imagination. A writer can many times be like an experienced village *vaidya* who holds a wrist, feels the pulse and diagnoses the disease in an instant what many physicians with a series of tests on ultra-modern machines fail to find out. The writer knows exactly which character in a given situation will behave in a particular way. One does not have to devote pages upon pages of psychological analysis of a character; a word, a phrase, even a glint in the eye is enough to reveal his intentions. Just one grain can show that the rice is cooked.

Dialogues in Indian fiction in English have occasionally been a problem, particularly when concerned with non-English-speaking people. Having been born and brought up in a village, I saw the elderly people conversing effortlessly in a native dialect which was pictorial, idiomatic and alive. It throbbed with life and wisdom. These dialogues remain my priceless possession even today. I have often endeavored to re-create them in English, avoiding the oddity which a literal translation often creates. In order to see that the dialogues are natural, I have learned my ears in many a secret place, listened to women talking about almost nothing for hours together, to the children who delightfully exchange idiocies as pearls of profound wisdom.

The fact that English is not the language of most of my characters has provoked some criticism. The objectors often forget that English is merely a medium of communication for the writer and a touch of artificiality is inevitable when characters and situations happen to be purely Indian, but it is no more than a momentary confusion. Once the reader has adjusted his vision, his understanding and his reflexes, once he has mentally aligned himself with the medium, everything becomes natural. After all, the problem is no different when a literary work of one language is translated into the other. One has to remember that it is largely through English that India and its literature have come to be well-known and understood outside and inside the entire country.

In the matter of point of view, I prefer the first person to the third person narrative because the former generates feeling of intimacy between the writer and the reader. While writing a novel or a short story, I identify myself with the first person narrator whether it be an old maidservant or a rag-picking boy and narrate everything as it might have happened to me. Of course, to overcome certain difficult situations which cannot be covered easily in the first person narrative, I switch to the omniscient point of view. I have often felt amused when some readers erroneously associate the "I" of the story with me as a person and laboriously discover similarities between the two, asking me whether I had written everything from *my* personal experience! I wonder what would they say about my novel *Neema: A Village Girl* which is in the first person narrative and the narrator happens to be a village girl!

A good short story touches a serious issue of life, what Henry Seidel Canby has called, "specific gravity." The story must not be merely an extended joke with a few twists and turns added to cheat the reader; it must take up serious issues of life – of men and manners, of hopes and frustrations. However, the treatment of serious issues by no means justifies an uninteresting and tiresome short story; its essential trait lies in being interesting. For a short story is the food that cannot go down the gullet without being palatable even if comprising all healthy and nutritive elements. I do not write merely for academics and scholars whose praise for a literary composition, as for a crossword puzzle, increases or decreases in proportion to the brain-teasing complexity it has or lacks. To read a good story is like going on a pleasant journey in the company of delightful personages who share an experience, exchange pleasantries, scour the gloomy cobwebs and end up by letting in a rejuvenating gust of fresh air. But to read a dull even if ingenious short story is like walking uphill with leaded shoes and the completion of each page gives one a feeling of a man-made obstacle tiresomely surmounted.

For some people to have a vein of humor in a literary work is to transgress the limits of serious writing. They do not realise that comic mode is an important aspect of life, enjoyed by all, even if only a few have been endowed with a vein of it. Humour demands of its writer a relaxed mood, a perfect control on the language and an immense capacity of playing upon words. All this is easy enough in a native tongue but difficult in a foreign language. It is creditable that among Indian short story writers, R.K. Narayan and Khushwant Singh have been successful in introducing, even in English, plenty of wit and humor which make their stories quite interesting and eminently readable.

A judicious use of not only humour but irony, suspense and narrative strategy can make a short story eminently readable. But sensationalism as a device to make a story interesting is to be avoided. Violence, sex and murder titillate the reader and make him go on with the story. However, to use them perpetually as mere baits is to addict the reader. Sensationalism in a short story is like chilies and spices in food; a little may add flavor but excess of them is injurious to health. A surfeit of sensationalism in Indian movies has spoiled the taste and dulled the sensibility of younger generation. Nothing can be a greater disservice to humanity than to dull the sensitivity of the people which weakens their empathy and makes them indulge heartlessly in violence, crime and murder. But as long as sensationalism originates from observed experience rather than from contrived situations, it fulfills an artistic requirement.

My own method has been to write a short story on any subject that happened to inspire me intensely. That is why the subjects varying from story to story are as diverse as love and infatuation, crime and punishment, materialism and spiritualism, poverty and riches, illusion and reality, villages and cities, and so on. Nothing is barred, nothing excluded. Some subjects may require a full-blown treatment; others merely suggestive and symbolic. I look around, watch, and re-create my impressions into words. Hence it differs from story to story. I could begin the story with vague hints of a character, a situation or a plot which become solidified into an image and which, in a polished form, are passed on to the reader. If I see a conflagration in a spark and an ocean in a bowlful of water, my effort would be to convey the impression in a more explicit manner to the reader.

In my stories, I captured a particular moment from the past or the present, shaped it to my needs, fashioned it to my likings, decked it in appropriate colors and fused it with life so that the story competes with the very life itself. The scene of action may be in New York or in New Delhi, the characters may be from the village or the city, but stripped of their peculiarities, they all embody various facets of life. Beneath their obvious dissimilarities, the same heart throbs and the same blood circulates in their veins. At some point of my life, each of these short stories had become a throbbing three-dimensional image which could not be kept away, and had to be given a creative outlet. For me, a short story is the concretised creative urge of the writer.

In this anthology, I have included short stories which might or might not conform to my above ideas in totality. "Perils of Simplicity" reflects my own dilemma when I lost many things because of my simplicity and hesitation. The two terms in the story "The Beauty and the Beast" meant respectively for human beings and animals in a circus become interchangeable. "A Memorable Present" shows an unusual gift of a student for his teacher. "The Bicycle" presents the pathetic picture of a father which eventually brings a dreamy son to his proper senses. "Different from Others" paints two contrasting pictures of the third gender one of which enthralls the narrator. "A Teacher of Humanity" is the authentic picture of the dentist Dr Mohinder Singh of Amritsar whose company imbibed in me the unforgettable traits of humanity. "Of Far and Near" is a tragic tale of a retired police constable deceptively deprived of his house by his own son. "Expiation" shows Vijaya's act of atonement for the sins of the family. "Corridor Therapy" illustrates how human company turns out to be best antidote for the dying old lady. In "A Great Prize," Chinamaya spends all his prize-money to secure a greater one. Literally and metaphorically, an act of "Sowing Seeds" pays rich devidends. "Blessed be the Dark" shows how one can transcend apartheid. "The Reconciliator" exemplifies how a small being can bring rapproachment among the warring factions. "The Holy Cow" shows the illtreatment of the eldest brother – a real holy cow – by an unholy one. "A Man of Gold" is the story of my childhood friend – a goldsmith – who showed his golden heart by saving my life at the risk of his own. "Amnesia" is a delightful yet realistic portrayal of an old forgetful couple.

No short story can be written by strictly adhering to its theory in totality. The characters are human beings who do not always move like pawns in the hands of their creator but have their own personalities with their likings and dislikings, whimsicalities and idiosyncracies. The wide world which I experienced – directly or vicariously – has been portrayed in the stories realistically with a tinge of wit and humour here and there to make them palatable. The characters have been chosen from all walks of life – teacher and student, potter and goldsmith, dentist and patient, the police officer and the constable, the rich and the poor, the old, the young and children,. The scenes are from the Punjab to Nagaland, from Delhi to Bihar, and so on. All I can say is: here is India's plenty.

Ramesh K. Srivastava

CONTENTS

1

PERILS OF SIMPLICITY

Feeling so deeply anguished, so much angry over Ruby Malhotra's deception in not marrying him even after two years of intimacy, Dayal Sharan did not utter a single word. It appeared that the stream of cool water to which he had traveled so laboriously in order to quench his thirst turned out to be a mirage. Finding Dayal immobile and silent, Ruby got up, shook him by holding his nose and said, "Sorry, my Bhole baba, forgive me for my false promises" and went out.

It was unambiguously clear that Dayal Sharan was made a fool, that with her bewitching beauty she had ensnared him to seek his help in mathematics. A feeling repeatedly invaded him to cry, to commit suicide but decided to consult his friend Niket Kaushik. Contrary to him, Niket was a versatile person with lots of knowledge. In a true sense, he was a worldly wise man who did not get swayed by emotions but like a judge evaluated things in their entire perspective. When Dayal Sharan informed him about Ruby's marriage, he said, "This was expected, Dayal, and I had forewarned you repeatedly of it. Now the best thing is either to get married with someone else or to divert your attention by doing some social work in which you are bound to remain surrounded by someone or other. The sorrow would be countered by the blessings and compliments of the people in general."

As Dayal remained silent, Niket continued after a pause. "Dayal, the first thing you have to do is to leave the city of Bhopal with which your romantic memories are associated. You can accompany me to Bina where I have been posted now. I know for sure that there is a vacancy of a Mathematics teacher in the Janata Inter College of the Labour Colony in Bina. I know its Principal and he had asked me to find some good Mathematics teacher from Bhopal Most of the students are very poor who can't afford private tuitions; hence the percentage of their failure is very high. Afterwards, they indulge in lawless activities. Hence besides teaching them, you'll be doing a great service to the poor. And remember Dayal, the rich may be thankless, but the poor remain obliged for life."

Five years passed. Dayal Sharan's job in the Janata Inter College and his stay in the Laborer Colony brought a miraculous transformation in him. He remained surrounded by the people of the colony – both parents and children – seeking advice on what was good for them, how to prepare for various competitive examinations and so on. When some of them succeeded in getting good jobs, they offered him sweets and touched his feet, expressing their gratitude that he had transformed their lives. They began to consider him a sort of god. During this time, Dayal became so much intimate with the people of the locality that even outside his college hours, he remained pleasantly preoccupied with their affairs. He too felt happy in their midst and forgot about Ruby's affair altogether as if it were a bad dream not worth remembering.

Many good proposals for his marriage began to come through his friend Niket Kaushik, but Dayal declined them all unwaveringly, saying, "I am not a misogynist, Niket. A woman's company pleases me but the fear of separation terrifies me. If Ruby-like separation happens again," he confided to him, "you may take it for sure that it would definitely be fatal. I have a very weak heart now."

One day when Dayal Sharan was happily enjoying on the occasion of Holi along with other people of the Labour Colony, a beautiful lady approached the crowd, asking for Dayal Sharan. Since the faces of most people were partly or wholly covered with colour and *gulal,* she failed to recognise him. When Dayal Sharan asked her, "Whom do you want?"

"Dayal Sharan, I am Ruby, your one-time friend. I had gone out five years ago."

"Oh Ruby! Now I recognise you," Dayal Sharan said somewhat surprised. "What do you want now?"

"Won't you take me to your house?" she asked.

Still staying there, almost fixed to the ground, Dayal Sharan remained unmoved as if he were paralysed momentarily and only when she reminded him again, did he agree to take her to his two-room quarters, saying, "Sorry Ruby, my room is in a mess.'

"I know, my Bhole Baba, that is part of your nature but I am happy that you are enjoying with these people."

"I find the people in this backward city of Bina friendlier and warmer than I had found them in the university or city of Bhopal. They provided balm to my wounded heart created by you. But for them, I would either have committed suicide or might have been in a mental asylum. But what brings you here? What can I do for you?"

"I am in deep trouble, Dayal," Ruby said, bringing a shade of sorrow over her shining face. "The pain I had given you is so serious that I cannot even beg you for forgiveness. But to show the genuineness of my feelings, I would do something which I never did to others before," and suddenly she sat down on the ground, held Dayal's feet, and placed her head over them.

"Don't do this Ruby," Dayal Sharan said, somewhat moved by her gesture. "I am all in a mess of Holi colours and cannot even raise and hug you, but sit down on the string cot, while I wash my face and hands. Afterwards we can talk at ease."

When they had sat down and taken tea, Ruby apologetically told him that her husband was cruel, that he thrashed her mercilessly everyday and that, unable to bear the torture any further, she had abandoned him. She expressed her desire for live-in-relationship with him.

"I have only these two small rooms with one of them as bed room, while the other is a sort of kitchen-cum-storeroom. How can you stay in such accommodation with me whereas you must have been used to luxurious living in London for five years. I take my meals at a roadside dhaba, which you won't like even to look at."

Ruby flashed her smile and came to him, hugged and kissed him, while he remained almost as a wooden figure, moving none of his limbs. "Don't you worry, my dearest Dayal, my Bhole Baba. I'll manage to live in such an accommodation because I know you have immeasurable wealth of love. All the expenses of eating and visiting places will be borne by me. I have a lot of money from my separated husband and my elder brother in Bhopal, my father having died two years back..."

"Then why don't you go to live with your brother?" Dayal asked.

"He is too domineering for me."

"You stay here for the time being," Dayal tried to reason with her. "Meanwhile, let me ask my close friend Niket about it."

When Dayal Sharan informed Niket Kaushik about Ruby, he was struck dumb and firmly advised him against her stay with him. "It is not her love or repentance for her past sins that brings her here but the utter selfishness. Don't fall into her trap again."

"What could she gain from me now?" Dayal innocently asked.

"I don't know that but Dayal tell her to stay in a hotel or with her brother but not with you. She might be involved in a crime and might have come for an incognito shelter. I warn you, Dayal. Don't let her stay or you'll repent and this time her deception might be fatal for you."

"But I can't turn her out, can I?"

"If you can't, then I will for you."

"No Niket. It will be highly discourteous. I cannot do so even to my enemies. She has after all been a one-time friend."

"And onetime deceiver."

❖❖❖

Dayal Sharan went over what had happened five years back. Ruby Malhotra was a Punjabi girl, very charming, vivacious and pleasant to talk to. She belonged to a rich family, her father being the owner of a huge readymade garments store in Bhopal. She was so beautiful that when she studied in the Barkatullah University at Bhopal in Madhya Pradesh, many students were after her but she had chosen to be with Dayal Sharan. The obvious reason to people was that Dayal Sharan was not only the handsomest of them all but very intelligent.

His love for Ruby Malhotra had taken place in a dramatic way. Whereas many boys were going around trying to befriend her, she had ignored all of them. Dayal Sharan was one person who never even looked at her. Interested in his studies, he did not nourish any romantic dream of going after beautiful girls.

His father was a simple farmer in a village where his upbringing took place. Hence for his studies, he often sat down in the library which provided a good atmosphere.

As he was studying in the library, Ruby Malhotra asked him, "Can I sit here?"

Dayal Sharan looked at her and said in a dry voice as if it were tape recorded, "This is library; everyone is welcome."

When Dayal Sharan got up, Ruby too got up and walked together out of the library, discussing some mathematical problems, raising eyebrows of other envious students. She had surprisingly chosen a person who, others derisively thought, did not even know how to dress properly.

As a token of gratitude for solving many of her mathematical problems, Ruby brought a beautiful necktie for Dayal Sharan, but he said, "I don't even know how to tie it."

"I'll come to your room and demonstrate it."

When Dayal Sharan tied the knot around his neck, Ruby laughed vigorously while he remained confused not knowing what had gone wrong. Ruby said, "You have tied the knot as one ties a cow." She held the necktie at its knot and dragged him around. Bringing his head close to her face and kissing him, she said, "You are my poor cow, my Bhole Baba!" After untying the knot which was very tight, she coolly said, "Dayal, a knot in the necktie has to be such that when you pull both ends of it, no knot is formed."

Dayal Sharan made many efforts to tie the knot under her direction and finally succeeded. In his happiness, he even began to jump like a monkey.

"Do you know Dayal why is the necktie put on by people?" Ruby asked and as he shook his head in the negative, she continued, "to wipe the nose off when it runs."

"Is that right?" Dayal asked innocently and began to bring the necktie closer to his nose.

Striking her fingers on his hand, Ruby checked him and then explained, "No. It is a part of a gentleman's dress." Pausing for a moment, she said, "You are such a wonderful fool! That is why I call you Bhole Baba."

"One more thing, Ruby," Dayal Sharan asked. "Is it true that the necktie is a sign of Christianity? In such a case, I would not like to wear it."

"No. It is just an item of dress which people of all religions use."

Ruby had come to realise that Dayal Sharan, because of his rural background, did not have much knowledge about the world but was good in Mathematics and hence decided to make full use of his expertise. If need be, Ruby stayed on in his room till late hours in the night to understand some mathematical problems. Dayal Sharan felt ecstatic pleasure in her proximity while explaining the problems to her. This continued for two years!

As the final examination was approaching, some students asked her, partly in fun, "When are you going to marry?"

Being clever, Ruby gave an evasive answer, "After the declaration of the result."

When Dayal was asked about it, he said, "Everything depends on Ruby."

Since Dayal had a lurking doubt about Ruby's marriage with him, he often talked about it with his friend Niket Kaushik but the latter said categorically, "I have told you many times that she would never marry you, Dayal. Take my word for it."

"Why do you doubt it when she loves me so much?" Dayal Sharan asked.

"She is good in Mathematics," Niket laughed, "and hence may be quite calculating."

After the result was declared, Ruby Malhotra obtained ninety percent marks in Mathematics which gave her not only the first position in M.A. but a gold medal for topping the faculty. It was surprising for most people that Dayal, who was more intelligent of the two and was teaching Ruby all these two years, got the second position with 88 percent of marks. It was obvious that in helping her, he had sacrificed his own interests.

When Ruby brought her wedding invitation card, Dayal Sharan found that she was getting married to the son of a textile mill owner in England. The date, place, time – everything was clearly spelled out with no scope for confusion. Like a dog who has been badly kicked while being tempted with a piece of bread, Dayal felt like abusing her for raising his hopes of marriage with her and then dashing them down. His silence was disturbed when Ruby asked, "Please do attend the marriage."

❖❖❖

Now remembering what had happened five years back, Dayal felt convinced by his friend's suggestion of not letting her stay with him. Instead of denying her categorically, he thought of some excuse, but none was readily available which could come to his rescue. Then he thought of one and said, "Ruby, I can't let you stay with me because my father is going to come to live with me."

"My Bhole Baba, you don't even know how to make an excuse," Ruby laughed. "I know your father died last year. I have been out of India for five years but have been keeping track of all your activities because of my love for you. This time I'll give you so much pleasure of my company that you'll forget the past."

Finding no other excuse, he allowed her – or rather she forced herself to stay with him. She got the string cot replaced by a little broader bed for sleeping together. Both lived almost as husband and wife, sleeping together on the same bed, going together for a walk, moving around the city and its parks, occasionally going to Bhopal, recalling old days but Dayal

Sharan told her that he did not want to remember the old days which reminded him of her treachery.

For six months, they continued to live together. The happiness that Ruby gave him now had wiped out all the hard feelings and anguish she had given earlier. If she had deceived him in the past, she compensated adequately by giving him heavenly happiness now.

One day on his return from the college, he found that Ruby had vacated the house with her bag and baggage, leaving a letter on the bed, requesting him to meet her at the Bina railway station. She was to catch the 18.30 train for New Delhi. Dayal consulted Niket Kaushik about it and he advised him that since it was to be the last meeting even though she had cheated him for the second time, there was no harm in going there.

The reservation of Ruby and her husband was in AC 2 Tier. The train was at the station but the TTE was not there. Ruby introduced her husband who warmly shook hand with Dayal, saying, "Both of us shall remain obliged for life for your contribution to us."

Ruby added, "He has been a great benefactor in my student days also."

The TTE came in his uniform, stood in the doorway of the compartment, demanding tickets before letting the passengers into the coach. A fine breeze was blowing. Ruby opened her purse, brought out the ticket and gave it to the TTE but before he could catch, it was blown away by the breeze. It took some somersaults and then through the gap between the platform and the train, slipped to fall on the railway track.

"What's to be done now?" Ruby asked the TTE.

"You can't get in the compartment unless you have a ticket."

"But I had given it to you," Ruby insisted.

"No. You tried to but I didn't get it. Either you pay up the charges from its originating station or get it from below the train."

Ruby peeped through the opening between the platform and the train and found the place to be quite dirty. The train had already given a whistle. She looked at Dayal Sharan like a beggar who was eyeing a piece of bread but being crippled could not pick it up himself, yet she said nothing. "How much would the charges be?" Ruby asked the TTE.

"I'll have to calculate," the TTE said. "But since it will be a new ticket, you might be waitlisted and disallowed. Another option is, if you want, you can go to the booking counter and get the duplicate ticket on payment of 25 percent of the cost of ticket."

"But meanwhile the train would leave which would mean missing my flight from New Delhi to London."

"Well, the choice is yours."

Meanwhile, the train gave the second short whistle which was an indication that within a couple of seconds it was about to leave and almost simultaneously a voice from the gap between the train and the platform said, "Take the ticket" and a hand was seen by Ruby. It was Dayal Sharan who was handing over the ticket. He was under the train.

Taking the ticket from his hand, Ruby and her husband yelled, "Thanks Dayal. Now lie down below the train between the tracks. Be quick. The train is about to move any moment."

As they finished the sentence and boarded the compartment, the train began to move – first very slowly and then caught up the speed. After the train had gone, the crowd noticed from the platform that a body lay on one side of the railway track, sliced up into two like a cucumber. The railway police was called.

While the body was being taken for post mortem, a paper was found in his pocket which read like this:

My dear Dayal:

I don't have the courage to face you after having deceived you for the second time, though let me assure you, there won't be the third time. My husband was neither cruel, nor divorced by me. During the last five years of our marriage, I did not conceive. We had the option of either adopting a child or having one by IVF technique. My husband wanted a natural one from my womb conceived in love and hence he sent me to you – my old lover – and I conceived as he wanted. Now I carry your seed in my womb as a token of love. Even though you had warned me that if I happened to desert you again, you would not survive, but I am sure you'll not fritter away your precious life uselessly. Of course, I bid you good bye for the last time. My husband and I will be leaving for New Delhi by Howrah Mail at 18.30. Please come to the station so that my husband and I could see and thank you personally for the last time.

Yours lovingly,

Ruby

The newspapers reported the next day that Dayal Sharan committed suicide as a result of his frustration in love.

❖❖❖

2

THE BEAUTY AND THE BEAST

Teeshee was a small girl of five, as small as her name was. She was from a village named Bagaira near Kathamandu in Nepal though the family worked and lived in a small factory in Agra. After her parents' death in a car accident, she had none to look after – no uncle, no aunt, no cousin. Very fair complexioned and with tiny limbs, the ill-fated girl aroused a momentary compassion in the onlooker's heart but none could do anything to help her. Her grandmother felt pity over Teeshee's fate and began to keep her. After five years when she too found it difficult to sustain the family, she was advised to put the girl in an orphanage. Hearing of it, Teeshee cried bitterly and refused to leave her grandmother.

"What a beautiful girl!" a man sitting in the orphanage remarked. "Why is she crying so badly?"

Her grandmother explained, "Teeshee is an unlucky girl. She ate up her parents when she was five. I kept her for five years but now when I don't earn enough, many times both of us have to remain hungry. I am a tree on the river bank – today here, tomorrow nowhere. Soon there would be dragon-flies hovering over this young beautiful flower and I have no means of securing her safety. I have come here to keep her in this orphanage and that is why she is crying."

The visitor was a middle-aged man. He looked at the girl and then the old lady and said, "The girl is exceedingly beautiful and appears no more than nine or ten. Such a girl can do wonders in a circus. We need a girl like her in our circus. I had come here to look for one in this orphanage. I am glad I met you. If you want, I can talk about her with my boss. Can you bring her to the circus tomorrow? Ask anyone for Billoo Ustad or the Ring Master and he will bring you to me. Meanwhile, I'll sound my boss."

"May God bless you," the grandmother said. "I'll never forget your goodness for life if you take Teeshee in the circus. It might make her life worthwhile. Otherwise, one doesn't know what will happen to this girl in this bad world!"

The next day, Teeshee with her grandmother went to the circus and was fascinated by the posters displayed all over the place – of girls on the trapeze as also of parrots, monkeys, elephants and tiger in humanised forms performing various tricks. Teeshee got momentarily mesmerised by them, saying, "I want to see the circus, granny."

"There is no money to buy poison, let alone circus tickets, Teeshee. Let us see the Ring Master. If he finds a job for you even if it is to wash the plates and to sweep the floor, you can make your life worthwhile. Then you can also see the circus everyday." Crying till now, Teeshee had a glint in her eyes. As if to encourage her further, the old woman said, "You will also have beautiful clothes and delicious food and that too bellyful."

Ring Master Billoo Ustad took both of them to Shishu Pal who was the Manager of the Universal Circus. When he motioned Teeshee to come to him, she cried bitterly by looking at his large body in a leather jacket with a dark hat, steely boots, and a black, leather whip. Seeing his terrifying personality and a dacoit-like pair of thick mustachios, she clung herself to the grandmother as would a monkey's child to its mother, fearing to be snatched away. Holding Teeshee's hands, he scrutinised her as if she were a goat or a chicken to be cut, cooked and eaten, calculating how much meat the body carried. He pressed her hands, her neck, her cheeks, her thighs and ankles, and told the old woman, "Bring her tomorrow in very little clothes; all her remaining clothes can be brought in a separate bag. I will have to scrutinise her minutely whether she is fit for the circus job or not. If I find her suitable, I'll keep her here and pay some money to you."

"It doesn't matter whether you pay me or not, but do treat her well. She is an orphan whom I have cared for five years."

The next day Teeshee and her grandmother were taken to a small improvised room of the Manager under a large tent where Shishu Pal asked the girl to become completely naked. Teeshee cried again, looking very pathetically at her grandmother. The latter too had a look of horror in her eyes but said nothing. The Manager hit the ground loudly with his leather whip creating a terrifying whistling and screeching sound. He repeated his order to remove all her clothes again but she hesitated still. Then on a hint from the grandmother and with her help, the Manager removed all Teeshee's clothes as if readying her for skinning. She went on crying while Shishu Pal pressed all parts of her naked body including her tiny breasts. Afterwards, he asked her to put on her clothes again, gave the grandmother an envelope containing one thousand rupees and told the latter to go.

"Can I visit Teeshee whenever I want?" the grandmother asked.

"Yes you can, but we are here only for fifteen days. Afterwards we shall go to the south."

That very night, Shishu Pal brutally bit Teeshee's soft meaty cheeks and pressed her bubbly breasts so hard as if clawing to take them out of her body. Then in a fit of excitement, he pressed his teeth around them, muffling her cries. Dismissing her protests and physical resistance, he violently raped the shrieking girl. In the morning, Teeshee was made to accompany two other girls who were already performing on the trapeze. He asked them to train Teeshee for it. With her light body and soft, supple limbs, Teeshee appeared to be an ideal girl for the trapeze. After a couple of days, she became friendly with the two girls Shivangi and Deepanshi. When Teeshee complained to them that Shishu Pal raped her frequently, they said the same treatment was meted out to them as well when they had come. Occasionally, he still called the one or the other for this purpose.

"Why don't you oppose him?" Teeshee asked.

"Can YOU oppose him?" Shivangi asked.

"No," Teeshee confessed in a dying tone. "He will throw me out and there is none in the world where I can go."

"That is the problem with all of us," Deepanshi said. "We have no alternative."

Among the three, Teeshee was the smallest and the most beautiful of all. As Teeshee went up in the air in dazzling fluorescent lights in her red bikini, her white body shone, like that of a mythical fairy. Besides, with the passage of time, she began to outperform the other two girls because of her small, nimble parts and light, almost moldable body. After going high in the air with the help of the swing, Teeshee's hands were taken by the other girl or she herself managed to catch the swing bar but not before she had taken two or three somersaults in the air. Consequently, she got the biggest applause from the public.

One day Deepanshi asked, "Teeshee, why don't you oppose your exploitation by the boss now? You are a darling of the people and as a startling beauty, you have become indispensable for the circus."

"I would have liked to do so, Deepanshi, but he threatens that after two or three somersaults as I seek your hands or the rod of the swing, he simply has to pressurise one of you to keep your hands or the swing bar a few inches away from my hands and that would be the end of me. When I fall down from that height not only might I die but worse, I would be maimed for life."

"Teeshee," Shivangi said. "I am glad you understand everything now."

While Teeshee's popularity among the raving people and the comments about her work in the newspapers made her very happy, her continuing brutal exploitation by Shishu Pal made the fire of hatred perpetually burning within her. She told him many times that she was tired, that she was not denying him sex but her limbs kept aching for the whole day and affected her efficiency in the trapeze and even disturbed her mental equilibrium but he remained unmoved. As if this was not enough, one day he asked her to familiarise herself with the circus animals, particularly the tiger and the elephants.

"When there is already Billoo Ustad for this work, why do you want me to familiarise with the animals?" Teeshee asked.

"So that when you defy me, I could ask the tiger or the elephant to kill you," and Shishu Pal laughed. Then lowering his tone, he said, "I want every player here to be all-rounded – knowing every other job. Of course, only girls work on the trapese but out of them I want you to learn the taming of these three large animals – a tiger and two elephants, hence it would be a new attraction to have a beautiful girl taming the beast – a good slogan to bring the beauty and the beast together."

Much against her wishes, Teeshee was forced to accompany Shishu Pal in order to familiarise herself with the animals, though she remained mortally scared of them for fear of being disfigured rather than for her death. If the tiger struck its paw over her one eye, one ear or even one cheek, her beauty would be spoiled forever. She did not mind dying, for it meant escape from Shishu Pal's exploitation, but to be deformed for life was unbearable.

When Teeshee showed her reluctance, Shishu Pal thrashed her with a leather whip. Giving her the choice, "You either have ten whip lashes everyday or learn to tame the animals."

It was a very hard choice. With tears in her eyes and cursing her fate, Teeshee agreed to go with him to the animals. They obviously appeared scared of Shishu Pal holding a leather whip and an electric prod. Hence though they roared and trumpeted, they seemed to grudgingly obey Shishu Pal, scared of the punishment from him.

Teeshee remained so much afraid of both Shishu Pal and the wild animals that she found no difference among them. Her fears brought nervousness in her which became counter productive and she could learn nothing about taming them. When she told her problem to Billoo Ustad, he promised to help her. In Shishu Pal's absence, he gradually took Teeshee to the wild animals, persuaded her to give them feed and soon a day came when she began to feed them with her own hands and even to touch some parts of their bodies. As the tiny, beautiful Teeshee with her petal-soft palm and fingers touched the tiger and the two elephants softly, they felt as if she were applying balm to their bodies. Her touches seemed to smother their beastly traits and brought out their kinder forms. The tiger gradually began to look at Teeshee with raised eyes, shook its ears, made friendly chuff-chuff sounds and then turned its face quietly back. The elephants, particularly the bigger one called Gajaraj, fluttered its ears and when it became more familiar with her, it raised its trunk and kept its tip on her head as if in benediction.

Excited and jubilant, Teeshee began to learn fast with the help of Billoo Ustad and found that the animals were responding well to her. As she remained more and more with them, she found a strange kinship with them and identified them with herself while earlier she used to associate them with Shishu Pal.

Now Teeshee had spent two years in the circus, had matured a little, though her body still remained slim and small, except that her breasts had begun to be somewhat visible. When Teeshee became an expert in making animals play dangerous roles, she became very happy. She told gleefully in glowing terms to Shishu Pal, "Sir, what you with your leather whip and abusive words could not do, Billoo Ustad did it so easily with kind words and loving treatment."

"Has Billoo Ustad fallen in love with you?" Shishu Pal gasped in suspicion. "In such a case, I'll have to throw him out of the circus."

Somewhat shocked, Teeshee said, "What do you say, sir! He is of the age of my grandfather! I am twelve while he is past 50. How could you think of such a relationship?"

"I thought because he takes personal interest in training you."

"You also take personal interest in training me."

"Your tongue has become quite active now," Shishu Pal scolded. "I'll have to train you how to talk to me." Taking the leather whip, he struck her two or three times, till she tearfully apologised and promised never to answer him back. Folding his whip, Shishu Pal finally warned, "Remember Teeshee, I am the boss of the circus. And don't forget to come to my camp tonight."

That night, Shishu Pal used her brutally. Being somewhat sadistic, he bit her cheeks and breasts besides thrashing her with his leather whip. She cried, begged, cringed but the man remained unresponsive. His thrashing and sex added one more layer of her hatred against him and she prayed earnestly to god that someday he would die or get killed.

One day, she asked Billoo Ustad, "Why is Shishu Pal so cruel? Has he always been like that?"

Billoo Ustad remained quiet for sometime and said, "I may tell you, my daughter, on condition that you would not tell anyone about it." When Teeshee assured him of confidentiality, he continued, "Shishu Pal is very very cruel. He is no different from Shishu Pal of *Mahabharata* who was killed by Lord Krishna. On a little quarrel with the then owner of the Universal Circus, he got him killed through a lion of the circus and became its owner. The old owner was his own elder brother. He was a real, gentle person, but no one raised a finger against Shishu Pal, because it was done through the lion, and hence no blame could be put on him."

"How was it done?"

"In one of the shows, Shishu Pal's elder brother was sitting in the lion's lap while the beast held his neck in its jaws. It was a great moment of suspense which people watched with fingers in their mouths. The next moment, the lion would invariably withdraw and the audience would clap thunderously. In my absence, Shishu Pal used to give food as well as commands to the lion. Hence when it put the neck of his brother into its mouth, Shishu Pal said, 'Chew it' and the lion chewed his neck. It was reported as an accident and that way Shishu Pal became its owner. Afterwards, Shishu Pal sold that lion, purchased a tiger and did not allow anyone to play that game. He took precaution so that none could do the same trick on him."

Both of them remained quiet for sometime, allowing Shishu Pal's act of cruelty to sink in them. They looked towards each other exchanging glances in disapproval of Shishu Pal's act.

Teeshee had now got perfection in the trapeze and was also making progress in managing some animal tricks in the circus. While talking with the other two girls Shivangi and Deepanshi, she found that they were as much unhappy with Shishu Pal's exploitation and cruelty as she was. Whenever any one of them complained to Shishu Pal against her exploitation, he always threatened that he would push her before one of the elephants or the tiger and that would be her end. The financial requirement forced them to bear everything silently till they could find another job and that was not easy. It was not surprising that all of them prayed for the beast's death in order to get some relief.

In the midst of all-round cruelty and exploitation, Teeshee felt really happy in the company of animals. They appeared so beautiful and so humanised. She spent some of her own money and occasionally purchased guavas, bananas and other fruits for feeding the parrots, monkey and elephants. While Billoo Ustad often fed the tiger from afar by throwing pieces of meat to it, Teeshee, on the contrary, fed most of them with her own hands. She found a strange pleasure in placing pieces of fruits on her palm before the monkeys while she gave green chilies to the parrots who nibbled them slowly while shrieking sweetly "Teeshee! Teeshee!!." Taking each bite of a carrot, a banana or a guava, the monkeys jumped all over the cage muttering something as if they were professing love to Teeshee. Even as she fed the tiger and the elephants, their soft mumbling sounds appeared as if in approval of her act of feeding them. When the tiger licked her fingers before grabbing the piece of meat, Teeshee became quite excited as if it were a show of its affection and love to her which was never done by the sex-hungry Shishu

Pal. The elephant Gajaraj beckoned her and with the help of its trunk made her sit on its back.

Many times when Teeshee was alone, she went to Gajaraj and talked to him while feeding him with sugarcane and *peepal* leaves with her own hands and he appeared to enjoy her company. "Gajaraj," Teeshee said, "sometimes I feel so upset, so miserable that I feel like committing suicide as there is no one whom I can call really mine."

Gajaraj made some kind of grunting sound and shook his head sideways a number of times as if he were disapproving the idea of her suicide. Understanding his answer, Teeshee said, "Gajaraj, what is the use of this life? I don't have any friend to whom I could show my bleeding heart from Shishu Pal's sexual exploitation. Everyone is mortally scared of him."

Stopping chewing midway, Gajaraj advanced a little, touched her head with its trunk and then brought it between its forelegs while he shook his head upside down, like human beings, as if in a positive manner. Taking the hint, Teeshee said, "I understand you, Gajaraj, that you are there. But what can I do? Sometimes I feel so disturbed, lose so much equilibrium of my mind that I begin to do funny things. The other day I was wrongly feeding meat to the monkeys and fruits to the tiger! Other girls consider me crazy and laugh at me when I come to have your company. Honestly Gajaraj, I find you much more human than that beast who goes around masquerading as a human being."

When the news of Teeshee's camaraderie with animals, particularly with the elephant Gajaraj, reached Shishu Pal, he was very happy. For emergency, particularly during Billoo Ustad'a absence, Teeshee could show various tricks of animals to the audience.

Even though Teeshee was doing a good job both at the trapeze and in showing the elephants' tricks, her exploitation by Shishu Pal continued. The only consolation she had was that its frequency decreased. She wondered many times what kind of man was he who was treating her worse than would the animals!

One night somewhat in anger, Teeshee muttered, "Sometime I feel that the only way to escape this torture from you is to kill myself or...?"

"Or what?"

She remained quiet and Shishu Pal asked again, "Or what?"

"To kill you," she finally muttered.

Shishu Pal laughed a laughter of devils and slapping her so hard on the cheek that she staggered and was about to fall when he said, "The day you even think of it, I will feed you to the tiger. You don't know how dangerous I am! My elder brother was nasty to me and I fed him to the lion in the circus. Don't ever entertain such nonsensical ideas or they will be your ruin."

A delayed realisation dawned on her that she should not have uttered such a thing, but she detested him so much that she could not control her tongue. Apologising to him, she went away to the animals. They appeared so much in playful mood with her and their faces appeared so beautiful, so warm and above all so human that many times she felt like opening the cage in order to sit in the company of the monkeys and the tiger. With her parents dead in her early age, she did not know the warm touches of parents' love but she had its inkling in the company of monkeys, the tiger and Gajaraj.

Occasionally, Teeshee accompanied Billoo Ustad in showing the feats of these animals to the public. Shishu Pal saw that Teeshee, being a short-statured, slim, beautiful girl, appealed to the audience much more than did Billoo Ustad. Since the demand of Billoo Ustad for higher wages was increasing, he felt happy in having at least one more person to use as a lever to counter the Ustad's demands.

Teeshee not only enjoyed her work but began to make the tiger and elephants do the feats with much more ease than Billoo Ustad could. Though she always carried the leather whip and the electric prod in case of emergency, an occasion for their use never arose. The audience liked the feats of the tiger and elephants, particularly when the tiger kept its paws on Shishu Pal's shoulders after garlanding his head. The audience gave a thunderous applause when the tiger got down from him and Shishu Pal walked safely away.

The last feats were those of elephants. The two elephants played many tricks including football. Shishu Pal fondly sat cross-legged on a red velvety carpet while both elephants kept their unburdening forefeet on his shoulders and garlanded him with their trunks, the kind they are seen in pictures on Deepawali occasion garlanding the goddess Lakshmi. It gave Shishu Pal an ecstatic pleasure as he imagined himself the god of the Universal Circus. Now only the giant elephant Gajaraj was left out for his solo feats. A large-sized green coconut was placed before him. First of all, he played with it as if it were a football, pushing and chasing it. Then on a hint from Teeshee, he checked its movement and placed his forefeet on it and nothing happened, but the moment Teeshee said, "Crush it," it was crushed flat while its water and its white kernel spilled all around. Then a giant but delicate full-blown transparent balloon was placed before Gajaraj on which he kept both his forefeet and yet nothing happened to it. Despite Gajaraj's heavy weight, the balloon stayed intact. When Teeshee said, "Crush it," it exploded with a loud sound. Finally, he was asked to perform another feat. This was the last item and the most dangerous of all. Billoo Ustad would normally lie down on the ground. Gajaraj would cover Billoo Ustad's entire body from feet to head with its own, and then keep both the heavy forelegs on the Ustad's head but without any weight and then after a few seconds, he would be asked to get down. Billoo Ustad would walk away without a scratch on his head. He would bow a number of times before the spectators who clapped thunderously while going out of the giant tent on the completion of the circus feats.

The circus show could not be considered complete without Gajaraj's last feat with Billoo Ustad. The problem now was that he was out of town while the audience was demanding the feat insistently. Seeing the mood of the audience, Teeshee suddenly announced, "Now Shishu Pal will lie down and Gajaraj would keep his forefeet over the head."

For a split second, Shishu Pal hesitated but the next moment seeing the audience restive, he lay down on the ground, eyeing Teeshee pathetically with fear and frown appearing alternately on his face. Gajaraj, covering Shishu Pal's entire body with his own, kept both his forefeet on the head of Shishu Pal without putting any weight. As the audience clapped and Shishu Pal looked anxiously around Teeshee, she said, "Crush it."

Before the sense of the order could go into fearful Shishu Pal's head, Gajaraj instantly put his pressure on the head, broke and flattened it with a terrible sound while the blood was splashed all around. The audience cried in horror while Teeshee remained dumbfounded.

❖❖❖

3

A MEMORABLE PRESENT

Each time Shashi Kant thought over the problem, he just could not believe how could it have happened! Even though he was captivated by Santara Devi's beauty, he had never dreamt of using her, let alone planning for it. How then could he be responsible for it? Nevertheless, he cannot deny the fact that the sexual act was committed with his teacher's wife. In any case, he felt that his mental peace could be obtained only after he had begged forgiveness from his teacher Rajguru.

He knew that Rajguru's wife Santara Devi was younger to her husband by ten years and that they had no issues. Probably it was this fact which was gnawing at Rajguru's vitals. On the contrary, Santara Devi was a cheerful woman with an ever captivating smile on her face. It never appeared to him that she had any pain or anguish in the absence of a child. Their temperaments, too, were contrastive. While Rajguru was introvert, confining himself to the world of books and the lab, Santara Devi was an extrovert – a fully bloomed flower nodding its head, dancing and singing, as it were, with the movement of breeze. A mere look at her refreshed the mood of the people.

One day Santara Devi asked Shashi Kant to persuade Professor Rajguru so that all three of them could go to see a popular movie. Normally, Rajguru was not inclined for such activities. Since Shashi Kant, being his research scholar, was very close to him, he agreed to his student's request. All three of them went to a movie which was very entertaining. Even in the dark, Shashi Kant could see Santara Devi's pearl-white teeth flashing as she laughed vigorously on funny situations. Her laughter was sonorous music to his ears. He did not know what happened but when the show was over, Rajguru was nowhere to be found. He was searched everywhere but in vain.

On reaching home, they found Rajguru sitting in a sullen mood in front of his quarters. Seeing them, he asked his wife Santara Devi, "Where did you go? I asked the neighbours and none could tell. At least you should have left a note or the key with the neighbours."

Santara and Shashi Kant looked at each other. He was going to tell his professor about his absence in the movie, but she put her finger on her lips to indicate that he was to say nothing to him. After they had gone inside and when Rajguru was made comfortable and at ease, Santara slowly held his nose in her fingers, shook it lovingly and said, "All three of us – you, me and Shashi – had gone to see a movie in Kailash theatre, but you came out in the middle and reached home. We went on looking for you in the intermission and then at the end of the movie but you were nowhere to be found."

Rajguru scratched his head somewhat puzzled and innocently asked, "Is that right?" and then after a pause, he laughed a little like a child, saying, "Yes. Now I remember it."

Many times Shashi Kant thought what a mismatched couple they were! She was like a green vine with multi-colored flowers wrapped around a near-dry tree. Since Shashi Kant was a bachelor, he had natural attraction towards Santara Devi but it was soaked with a heightened sense of ennobled feeling, close to worshipping her. The feeling that she was his teacher's wife whose place was equivalent to a goddess was never allowed even for a moment to be forgotten. When thoughts contrary to it intruded in his mind, particularly after seeing her bewitching beauty, he brushed them aside. But many times it happens that the more one removes an idea, the more does it come insistently like the pain of a missed opportunity. Whenever Santara Devi wanted to go for shopping, Rajguru would say, "Take Shashi Kant with you."

Shashi Kant was good in every respect and knew which items were available at which place. There was hardly anything that he did not know – movies, theatres, restaurants, shopping places – and he felt genuine pleasure in helping Santara in every respect imagining that in helping her he was helping his professor, particularly when Rajguru had no time or interest in these things. Such things were a burden to him.

Had Santara Devi been aged or had he been an adolescent, the problem would not have arisen. Now in his young age, he had a feeling that by being attracted towards her, he was doing something improper, something immoral and unwise, though despite it, he could not resist being drawn emotionally towards her. As a matter of fact, she was so vivacious, so beautiful and so richly endowed that he looked forward to the occasion when he would be asked to accompany her for an outing. The onslaught of such feelings made Shashi Kant very uneasy.

Even though he had no any desire for sexual gratification with her because such an idea was unimaginable, even repugnant to him, something was pulling him to her. For this even Rajguru too was partly responsible. It appeared from his attitude and facial expression as if to unhinge him from his introvert, bookish cell required Herculean energy and in its absence he remained gladly glued to it.

Though Rajguru had given all the freedom to Santara Devi to go with Shashi Kant anywhere anytime, when Rajguru went out of station in meetings of selection committee or practical, Santara Devi went out more frequently with Shashi Kant – to restaurant, to her friends' houses, even to see movies. Probably being alone, she felt the house a sort of suffocating confinement she wished to avoid. She was like a bird who would like to flutter her wings and to chirp noisily with others. On these outings, whenever Santara's body accidentally came in contact with his, he felt as if an electric current had coursed through his entire body, as if the rubbing of two dry bamboo sticks had created a powerful spark and it was difficult for him to become completely normal, though nothing unusual was seen on Santara's face.

It was this veneration, this blind faith in the teacher in all classes, even in the college and the university, which remained with Shashi Kant all his life. For him, the words of his teacher were law, his lifestyle a model for emulation and his teachings inviolable principles. "The teacher can do no wrong," remained a motto permanently embedded in his mind and as a result he always had their blessings in abundance.

When Shashi Kant was in class five, the Head Master organised a function on the Teachers' Day in which students were asked many puzzling questions. Shashi Kant was asked, "Suppose you are in a boat with your mother and your favorite class teacher. The boat develops leakage and only two people could go in it. You have to drop either your mother or the class teacher. Whom would you throw in the river?"

Shashi Kant said he would throw his mother, leaving the class teacher in the boat. When asked for this reason, he explained that mother's love was laced with filial compulsions and self-interest, but that of the lady teacher was greater who loved and taught him, prepared him for life, knowing well that he might not see him again in life. There was a thunderous applause from all sides.

After completing his M.Sc. examination, Shashi Kant got registered for a Ph.D. degree in Physics under the supervision of Rajguru Prasad who was a Professor of Physics in Jabalpur University. He remained confined mostly to his research work and publications in the department as well as at home. In one room of the vast university residential quarters, he had set up a mini Physics laboratory in which he often remained preoccupied. He hailed from a place which was only six kilometers from Shashi Kant's village. His father knew the family of Rajguru and had requested the professor to act as his son's local guardian. It was a matter of privilege for Shashi Kant that he was working under Rajguru whose reputation as a scholar had spread far and wide. Since Shashi Kant had distinctions with over eighty percent marks in B.Sc. in all three subjects – Physics, Chemistry and Mathematics, his father had requested Rajguru to help him get admission in M.Sc. in Physics in the Jabalpur University so that after completing it, he would get a good job.

When Shashi Kant became a gold medalist in M.Sc., he began to do research under Rajguru's supervision. Because of the connection of the village and his old association, Shashi Kant revered his teacher the same way as he had his school teachers. He felt genuine pleasure in being of any service to him or his wife. Since Rajguru had no inclination to waste his time in household chores, such as, bringing vegetables, arranging wheat flour, paying electricity or water charges, bringing grocery and other items from the market and taking him or his wife to various places, Shashi Kant gladly performed them.

Now at twenty five, when Shashi Kant had a UGC Research Fellowship and life was running well, there was something that continued to bother him and he could not forget and forgive himself for the crime he had committed. Many times, he got up in the middle of the night and remained awake. The problem was that he could not consult any of his friends about it because the leakage of the secret could be disastrous to him and to her. What anguished his inner being most was that he had deceived someone who had complete faith in him. It was self-rapprochement which troubled him from which he could not rise.

Shashi Kant had repeatedly taken a commitment from Rajguru and Santara well in advance that the day the last formality of viva voce examination of his Ph.D. was over, they would accompany him for a dinner in a grand restaurant, see a movie and allow him to give them a very memorable present. Since all his success in M.Sc. and Ph.D. was due to Rajguru Prasad, he wanted to give such a present which would be a fitting remembrance as his *Guru Dakshina.* He had already thought of many items one of which could be the present but the final decision would have to be taken by the professor and his wife Santara together. Unfortunately, immediately after his viva voce examination, Rajguru had to leave the station to attend an important U.G.C. meeting in New Delhi. The information dampened Shashi Kant's spirits and he was on the verge of crying. Seeing him sad on the great day, Rajguru called Santara and told her to entertain Shashi Kant on his great day.

After Rajguru's departure, Santara Devi sat before Shashi Kant and said, "It does not look nice for you to remain so gloomy on this great day."

"What can I do? Rajguru sir has gone to New Delhi!"

Lifting his chin with her right hand, she asked him, "Would you like to take his *better half* for an outing?" emphasising the two words.

Shashi Kant gave a short laugh and said, "Have I ever dared to say no to what his better half ever commanded me to do?"

"But this is not a command, Shashi. It is just a friendly request as per Rajguru sir's wishes."

"My Guru's wife's request is more than a command for me," Shashi Kant said.

It was the month of October. Now evenings had become slightly cold. Shashi Kant was in his usual dress, while Santara Devi looked gorgeous in her light cream coloured chiffon saree. First of all they went to a grand restaurant and had a dinner. Afterwards, it was their turn for the movie. As they were sitting in the theatre lobby for the door of the balcony to be opened, someone commented rather audibly, "What a handsome couple."

Santara looked at Shashi Kant who in his agitated mood appeared to be on the point of quarreling with them but she pressed his hand lovingly and he became quiet. In the movie, Santara held his hand on the common handrest while a warm sensation continued to course through his veins.

When they came out of the movie, it was midnight and raining torrentially with thunder and lightning. Taking Santara's scooter out of the stand, Shashi Kant drove it while she sat on the pillion. With each draft of windy rain, their scooter got momentarily shaken but Santara kept encircling his waist strongly. When they reached her home, Shashi Kant's body was drenched to the bone, though inwardly it seemed as if on fire because of her prolonged warm company. His clothes were dripping with water and he had begun to sneeze. It was still raining heavily when Shashi Kant expressed his desire to go back to his hostel room in order to change his clothes to save himself from catching cold.

When Santara motioned him to stop for a moment, he asked her, "Do you have firewood, coal or heater so that I could dry up my clothes?"

"No. None of them, but first of all come and change your shoes and clothes," Santara said. She brought Rajguru's slippers and clothes, directing him to change them in the bathroom. Initially, he hesitated and said laughingly, though hiding his nervousness, "I am not yet great enough to be in Rajguru sir's shoes."

"These are not shoes but slippers and clothes. If you don't want to use Professor's clothes, would you like to be in my blouse and saree?" Then after a short laugh, she coaxed him, "Don't be fussy. Go and change them."

He was somewhat surprised that Rajguru's clothes fitted him well. Meanwhile, Santara too changed herself into a light pink gown. In her wet, loose hair and unadorned, natural face, she looked like a freshly bloomed flower with dew drops all over it. For a moment, he could not remove his glances from her simple yet captivating beauty. She brought a cup containing some syrup which was very strong and smelled like liquor. Shashi Kant hesitated a little and did not want to take it, but persuading him sweetly, Santara made him drink it, saying, "It will save you from catching cold. I too am going to have a cup of it." Then she led him to the bedroom, made him lie down under a quilt, kissed him on his forehead and said, "Lie down well tucked up in the quilt and have a good sleep, my little baby.

You'll be alright in the morning. Rajguru sir is not going to be back for the next two days."

In the morning, when Shashi Kant got up, he found himself in the same bed with Santara's naked body entwined around his. He realised that the dream that he had had of having sexual union with her was a reality now. He had committed a sinful act the same way as the mythical Chandrama had done by raping his teacher Brihaspati's wife Tara.

Shashi Kant quietly detached himself from her body, came to the bathroom, put on his own clothes, now dried, and without saying a word to the still-sleeping Santara, he came out of the house.

For one whole month and a half, Shashi Kant went on wandering from place to place in order to avoid both Santara and Rajguru. He did not have the courage to face Rajguru because he had been treacherous to his teacher. Since his stay in the city would have raised serious questions about his act of not meeting his teacher, particularly after completing his Ph.D., he remained in his village. Finally, when he did come stealthily to his hostel room, he was surprised to find an urgent message from Santara Devi, asking him to visit her house soon.

When Shashi Kant reached her home, he kept his eyes low, burdened with a sense of guilt. As Santara put her hand over his head, Shashi Kant bent low on her feet, and began to weep bitterly, saying, "I am guilty, madam, and would gladly accept any punishment you would give, though my sin is unpardonable."

Santara smiled broadly and said, "Let me tell you clearly that what had happened was not your fault, but a part of our plan, though it was accelerated by our cupfuls of scotch whisky."

Shashi Kant still failed to comprehend the sentence fully and obviously expected some more clarification. After she had made him seated on the sofa and wiped off his tears, Santara slowly began, "Prof Rajguru, after several medical tests, has been found to be incapable of fertilising me and, to cut the story short, what I did on that night had his consent. You will be happy to know that I have conceived. Once you had promised a memorable present to us after your Ph.D. I take it that way."

❖❖❖

4

SWEET REVELATIONS

Shekhar Sinha had come to Phagwara in Punjab from Bhagalpur in Bihar on transfer in a nationalised bank. Later on his wife Anshika also joined him after becoming a Lecturer in Botany in a local college. What both Shekhar and Anshika realised that unlike Biharis, people in Punjab were handsomer and fairer in complexion. Now they realised why so many Punjabis were working in Bollywood movies. Shekhar found women particularly attractive, even captivating. Gifted with beauty, they dressed well, lived cheerfully and did not mind doing menial jobs at various houses, such as, sweeping and mopping the floor and scrubbing utensils.

Charmed by their personalities, Shekhar could not resist momentarily thinking that if he were unmarried, he would not have minded marrying even one of these extremely beautiful maidservants. Now there was no point in repenting over it because he had a dark-complexioned wife from his own state who earned a handsome salary which made the family live a good life. Hence he must remain satisfied by simply looking at these beautiful girls.

It was the month of June when they had visitors from Bhagalpur – their cousin Amba Dutt and his son Vivek. Refusing to sit even for a minute, Amba Dutt said to Shekhar, "My son Vivek wished to spend a week of his summer vacation with you people in Punjab and hence I have brought him here. His school will reopen in July. Meanwhile, please take care of him. I would have stayed with you at least for the night but other people from Bihar are at the Phagwara railway station and we all have to go to Vaishno Devi by the train which soon will be there. My blessings and apologies to both of you. I promise to stay with you at least for a day when I come back in a week's time to take Vivek back to Bhagalpur."

Both Shekhar and Anshika convinced him, "Rest assured, we'll treat him well. You should have no worry about him."

"No worries at all," Amba Dutt said, "because this is his other home in Punjab. May God keep both of you happy."

Vivek was a seven-year old boy with a sharp mind and a cheerful temperament. While Shekhar and Anshika were talking with Amba Dutt, Vivek meanwhile went around the entire duplex house, inspecting each room on both floors. In no time, Vivek adjusted himself well with his uncle and aunt. After he had taken money for a chocolate from his uncle, he went around playing and then came back asking for money for one more chocolate which Shekhar refused, "One chocolate is all you'll get today from me."

Vivek remained quiet for sometime and then asked him, "Uncle, why do we have two eyes and two ears when one is good cnough?"

"So that if one does not work well, the other alternative is there."

"I wish I had two uncles," Vivek mumbled, half to himself but within the hearing of Shekhar.

Alarmed, Shekhar asked, "What makes you wish so?"

Somewhat coolly Vivek replied, "So that when one uncle refuses to give money for a chocolate, I could ask the other one!"

In no time, Vivek began to look for occasions when he could claim a chocolate either from his uncle or from aunt. Vivek noticed that though his uncle Shekhar was reading something, his eyes were looking surreptitiously at the maidservant Indu Rani, sweeping or mopping the floor. Of course, Shekhar's face remained fixed to the book but his eyes seemed to follow the movements of her body.

After the maidservant had gone and Anshika was upstairs, Vivek began with a mischievous look in his eyes, whispering to Shekhar, "Uncle! I don't know how to read a book without looking at it. Can you tell me how to do so?"

"That's an idiotic question," Shekhar snubbed him. "How can one read a book without looking at it?"

"But I saw Uncle that you were reading the book while your eyes were on Indu Rani aunty!"

"Sh! Sh! Sh!" Shekhar put his finger on his lips to indicate that he must not say such things. Vivek spread out his hand meaningfully to his uncle who handed him a ten-rupee note, saying, "You wanted this for a chocolate. Fetch and eat it upstairs where your aunty is learning about flower plants from the gardener Rajender. And don't say such things before others."

"I won't," Vivek said mischievously, "now that I have the money for a chocolate."

Anshika had kept a small garden on the terrace of their duplex house. She loved the flowers and their plants so much that she took a good care of them with the help of the gardener. Being Lecturer in Botany, she took particular interest in putting flags with the names of each plant so that visitors could appreciate and learn about them.

Vivek had no real interest in the plants or their flowers. When Shekhar sent him upstairs to see what his aunt and the gardener were doing, Shekhar's purpose was to snatch some romantic words and pleasantries with Indu Rani in the absence of Vivek. Gradually, Indu Rani also began to like her owner's appreciating eyes and said to him, "Sir ji. Could you bring a *parandi* for me? I don't get time to go to the market because of my work. I'll pay for it."

The next day, Shekhar brought a beautiful black *parandi* – a braid with three strands at the end of which were woven various patterns with gold threads. As if to see how the *parandi* looks like on her, Shekhar placed it casually on the back of her head, but the moment he did so, a giggle escaped from Vivek. Throwing the braid on her hand, Shekhar said, "It is quite good. You made a good buy."

As Shekhar began to read his book, Vivek quietly claimed a ten-rupee note from him.

Shekhar felt that Anshika was spending too much time on her terrace garden with Rajender Kumar who was quite handsome. Hence occasionally he sent Vivek upstairs stealthily to see what they were really doing. Vivek went upstairs and in no time came down visibly happy with a ten-rupee note and went out to buy a chocolate. Shekhar asked Anshika, "Do not pay money frequently to Vivek or else he will get spoiled."

Anshika said in irritation, "Is it I or you who spoil him? You give him money to go upstairs and see the beautiful flowers."

"I do so because he does not let me study here for my departmental examination."

"The same thing with me. When I want to take notes about flowers with the help of Rajender, Vivek disturbs me and I send him back to you or to the market."

Shekhar said laughingly, "Vivek cleverly exploits both of us."

One Sunday, Anshika was taking notes about her flowers when Vivek was disturbing her. She asked him, "Vivek, go very quietly and find out what your uncle is doing. The maidservant is also working downstairs. She might steal something."

After looking around everywhere, Vivek went to Aunt Anshika again and whispered in her ear that Shekhar was doing something with the maidservant and that if she gave him money for a chocolate, he would reveal the details. When she gave him a ten-rupee note, he said, "Uncle Shekhar was kissing her."

The next day Vivek came downstairs quietly with a mysterious smile, indicating that he had some juicy information and asked Shekhar, "Uncle, show me your palm."

"Why? Have you learnt palmistry?"

"Yes," Vivek said, taking his uncle's palm in his hand. "You have a wife whose name is Ankita. Your palm says that right now she is showing her palm to Rajinder uncle."

"Is that right?"

Still holding his uncle's palm, Vivek continued, "In order to get the answer to your query, you will have to deposit the prescribed fee with your nephew."

"Clever fellow!" Shekhar said, slapping him affectionately. "You are exploiting even your uncle."

Since Vivek was there only for a week of summer vacation, both of them did not mind paying such an amount. Now the week was nearly over but during this period both Shekhar and Anshika began to suspect each other of extra-marital relations which resulted in their tense faces and occasionally petty verbal exchanges. They did not want to have a big fight lest its report went to Vivek's parents in Bhagalpur and hence were postponing it for a period till his departure from their place.

The revelations that Vivek made before them had become more and more juicy day by day. He gave both of them nearly identical information – of amorous activities between Shekhar and Indu Rani, on one hand, and Rajender Kumar and Anshika on the other. They related to holding laldies' hands, the furrowing of their hair, touching of their cheeks, hugging and even kissing them. It was at this point that Anshika in her anger wanted to nail Shekhar down and said, "Vivek, my nephew, you are a good boy. You told me many things about your Uncle's affair with the maid. If you tell me everything in the presence of Shekhar what you had revealed to me at various times, I'll give you the biggest chocolate. Would you do so?"

"Why not?' Vivek gladly agreed. "That would be the sweetest revelation."

After that he went to Shekhar and asked him, "Uncle, I told you many things about Aunty and how uncle Rajinder behaves with her. If you promise me the biggest chocolate, I can tell everything on her face right in your presence."

Feeling happy, Shekhar said, "Vivek, if you do so, I'll give you not one but two biggest chocolates."

Vivek winked at him by narrowing his one eye and when he was somewhat jubilant, Anshika came downstairs and began, "Vivek, you're a very good boy. Would you tell on your Uncle's face what you have been telling me about goings on between your uncle and your aunty Indu Rani?"

"Yes, Aunty," Vivek said. "Uncle Shekhar has been doing with Aunty Indu Rani nearly everything what Uncle Rajender has been doing, Aunty, with you."

It was as if both heavy weight champions with their gloves on were ready to punch each other in the ring when Vivek had declared both the fighters disqualified. They stared with their blood-shot eyes at each other when Amba Dutt came with his luggage and sat down in the drawing room. After having usual courtesies, Amba Dutt asked, "I hope Vivek has not troubled you people." He waited for a moment and before any of them could say a word, he continued, "I forgot to warn you people in hurry that Vivek is addicted to chocolate-eating and for it he can tell a thousand lies and create serious misunderstandings and even quarrels between husband and wife. He had done it earlier in the houses of some relations where he had stayed in the past."

Shekhar and Anshika looked at each other. When their eyes searched for Vivek, he had disappeared.

❖❖❖

5

THE BICYCLE

Pandit Sukh Ram was a middle class Brahmin who wore his traditional dress of white *kurta* and *dhoti*, wooden sandals called *kharaun,* and displayed his long *choti* – a tuft of hair – over his shaven head as if it were a national flag. With a sandalwood tilak over his forehead, he could easily be identified from a distance as distinctly as would a man from outer space. He always carried a small home-stitched cloth bag which contained an almanac, a slate and a white chalk stick with which he made calculations of various stars, their positions and movements, and their significance in the lives of his anxious customers. Though in his middle fifties, Sukh Ram was not a very knowledgeable fortune-teller or a palmist, but for the village people, some little inane predictions of their good made them happy and they gave him away some money, wheat flour or rice. Their queries normally centered around the auspicious dates for someone's marriage or engagement, for sowing the seeds or even for the admission of children to school.

Somehow this way of living of his father did not appeal to his son Hari Lal. Many times when other students made fun of his father, he had no choice but to bear it with a feeling as if someone had squeezed his self-respect. What particularly irritated him was that his father had forced him to keep a shaven head with a long *choti* against his own wishes. Though his shaven head was hidden under a white cap, the *choti* invariably peeped from behind it, as if itching to come out of its confines. Some of the students mischievously pulled it from the right or the left side to tease him and he remained confused, looking like a fool this way and that but all in vain. When he told his father that his *choti* was creating a lot of problems for him and that he would like to cut it, Sukh Ram simply said, "The world has become devoid of religious and moral values. Have you not seen Lord Narad, how proudly he displays his *choti*? Hence never think of cutting it; just keep it under your cap." Then after a pause, he asked, "By the way, how do they trouble you?"

Hari Lal timidly began, "All the children from this village go to school on bicycles. I am the only boy who goes on foot. While riding the bicycles, they pull my *choti* from behind and by the time I look at them, they pedal away their bicycles and move forward. I have to quarrel with many students who have become my enemies now."

"I feel you too need a bicycle," Sukh Ram whispered to himself.

Unmindful of his father's mumblings, Hari Lal explained, "The students tease me in the class also. I have become a good laughing stock for them. Even the teachers to whom I complained too made fun of me."

"No matter what happens, you would not cut the *choti*," Pandit Sukh Ram threatened him with his waving staff, saying, "This has been our ancient heritage, mentioned in *Vedas* and *Puranas*. Tomorrow if they pass remarks against my *choti* and my shaven head, would you cut my head also?"

Now his wife Vidya Vati came on the scene and snatched the staff from her husband's hand and, throwing it away, angrily yelled, "Don't you feel ashamed of threatening a young son? He is not a child now. How does it matter if he wants to cut his *choti*? If all his class fellows don't have *chotis*, does it make them Muslims? Has he taken upon his shoulders the responsibility of preserving Hinduism? If you want to do anything funny, you may go ahead, but don't make my son an object of fun all around." She hugged the crying son, wiping off his tears.

"I have promised him a bicycle if he gets first class marks in the High School examination," Sukh Ram coolly asserted. "Then he wouldn't be on foot." After Hari Lal had left, Sukh Ram reminded his wife that after so many years of futile wait, his son Hari Lal's birth was the result of the boon given by Choti Baba who had exacted a solemn pledge from both of them that when the son is born, he would have to keep a *choti* till his marriage, failing which he will encounter innumerable difficulties. Vidya Vati confessed remembering it very well but she had knowingly kept a finger on her lips to keep him quiet as also to mollify the son.

Pandit Sukh Ram had consulted his friend Jagannath Tiwari of Jhalwan town about the cost of a bicycle as it was not available in his village. On finding out that it cost one hundred rupees, he realised, it was quite difficult for him to arrange so much of money for Hari Lal's bicycle. Sukh Ram remembered that over four decades back when he was an adolescent, the zamindar's son had come riding a bicycle in the village. The village people had seen it for the first time and were wonder-struck that such a contraption as a vehicle could exist at all! One of them had described the two-wheeler like this: "The zamindar's son was flying on a machine, moving on two wheels connected by a rod."

"How could that be possible?" another man had questioned. "He would obviously fall down. He must be taking the support of a staff or of his own feet to save himself from falling down?"

"He took no support at all, I tell you," the first person had asserted. "I have seen it with my own eyes."

The zamindar's son had often given rides to some boys as an occasional favour but with the condition that they would pedal it by sitting on the bicycle-carrier whereas he would balance its handle from his own seat. Many children gladly did so in order to have the pleasure of riding the bicycle. Sukh Ram, however, had stayed away from it.

As the time progressed, the bicycles began to be counted on fingers, the only difference being that earlier they used to carry the inscription of "Made in England" but now they were made in India. As some more years passed and his son Hari Lal began to go to school, more and more bicycles began to be purchased in the village.

Now nearly all of Hari Lal's class fellows going to school had their bicycles – old or new – except him. In order to put pressure on his father, he occasionally did not take meals, and his father Sukh Ram repeated his old promise of buying a bicycle after his High School examination.

"I don't believe in your promises any longer, Father," Hari Lal said. "You had also promised it earlier to me after my Eighth class but now even the High School examination is over. What is the guarantee that you'll buy it the day my result is declared and I pass the examination?"

Touching his holy thread and holding the hand of his friend Jagannath Tiwari as a witness, Sukh Ram promised, "If I don't buy you a bicycle after you pass your 10th class examination, you may call me a sweeper. Jagannath and Vidya Vati are witnesses to my promise."

Placing a reassuring hand over the boy's head, Jagannath Tiwari said, "I guarantee you, Hari Lal, that if he doesn't buy, I'll do it for you."

After Jagannath Tiwari had left, Hari Lal told his mother, "You are a witness, mother. If I don't get my bicycle, I will run away from home without telling anyone and then will also have my *choti* cut."

Many times, the students of the village made fun of Pandit Sukh Ram. When going out of the village, the Pandit rode over an old skeletal and tottering mare for his conveyance. As against his *kharaun* – wooden sandals – which he used in the village for going out of station, he would use a pair of old shoes having holes at the toes. His white cap too had a hole from which his clean-shaven pate was visible.

A month before Hari Lal's examination was to be over, he looked at the bicycles of others and said, "My father is going to buy a bicycle for me after the result of 10th class is declared."

"It is a good joke of the year," one student said and all others laughed because they knew that it was extremely difficult for the poor man like Sukh Ram to do so. He added, "I hope the bicycle too would be as well-ventillated as the liberally-holed shoes and cap of the Pandit are." And they all laughed again.

"Sukh Ram is not really that poor," another boy said. "He is just stingy. I saw him with a pair of silver anklets in a goldsmith's shop."

The revelation of having a pair of silver anklets shocked Hari Lal. He had seen his mother stealthily keeping the shining anklets into a velvet pouch. Sukh Ram was also seen taking rather extra care of his old mare, giving her a good feed, particularly a lot of grams as also a good bath, cleaning its well-padded saddle and polishing the leather strips of its reins.

Hari Lal asked, "Are you going out in some marriage?"

"No," Sukh Ram said. "Why?"

"Because you are taking a good care of the old mare and its items," Hari Lal said though he checked himself from referring to the mother's silver anklets.

Though Sukh Ram gave no reply, Hari Lal felt peeved against both his father and mother for indulging in non-essential, rather luxurious expenses while ignoring his basic need of a bicycle, the absence of which was causing him so much of humiliation.

Now only ten days were left for the result to be declared, but none of his parents talked of the bicycle. Worse still, the old tottering mare of his father died. Miser as his father was known, he did not spend money to buy another horse or mare for conveyance. Hari Lal felt momentary pity for his father who in his middle fifties had to trudge along rather long distances to go to different villages on foot even though occasionally his feet were found blistered and bleeding. The next moment, however, he dismissed such feelings because of his father's stinginess and his forgotten promise of buying him a bicycle.

When his result was declared, Hari Lal had first class in his High School examination whereas his other class fellows had either failed or passed in second and third divisions. He announced to his mother in jubilation, "I have passed in the first division, mother." He did not refer to the bicycle, just to see whether she or his father remembered it.

Jagannath Tiwari lived in the town of Jhalwan where Hari Lal studied from the sixth to the tenth class. Since the town was two miles away from the village, Jagannath Tiwari was made a sort of local guardian so that in case there were rains or the river was in spate, the boy could stay there for a couple of hours or even for a night.

Finding no bicycle even two days after the result was declared, Hari Lal quietly left for Jagannath's place in Jhalwan.

He informed Jagannath Tiwari of his result but didn't say a word about the bicycle. He was quite determined now that in order to spite his father, the first thing he would do is to cut his *choti*. He had saved a very small amount of money with which he decided to purchase a pair of tiny scissors to cut his *choti* which had all along appeared so anachronistic to him. As he was buying a pair of scissors, he saw in the adjacent shop a new bicycle being made ready. Temptingly and with entranced eyes, he observed the assembling process of the bicycle when someone kept his hand softly over his shoulder. It was Jagannath Tiwari.

"Do you like the bicycle," he asked Hari Lal who was eyeing the bicycle. "If you do, I'll buy it for you."

"Uncle, why make fun of me?" Hari Lal asked. "When my father failed to do so, how could you do it?"

"Because I had given you the guarantee," Jagannath Tiwari smilingly said, then looking at the shopkeeper, he asked, "How much money is still due?"

The shopkeeper said, "I needed one hundred rupees for the bike. An amount of seventy rupees has been adjusted against the sale of your old mare and twenty rupees for the pair of your silver anklets. Together they make ninety. Give me ten rupees more and the bicycle belongs to you."

As Jagannath Tiwari was about to give ten rupees to the shopkeeper, Hari Lal pulled him to one side. A sudden realisation dawned on him now that the old mare was not dead as he was informed earlier, but was sold as was his mother's silver anklets – all for his bicycle! He imagined that as he would proudly be riding a new bicycle in the village, the derisive eyes of the people would mockingly stare at him while his old father in torn shoes with blistered and bleeding feet would be seen wearily trudging from some remote village while his mother would futilely be covering her naked feet with the fringe of her saree.

"No uncle. No." Hari Lal pathetically but vehemently opposed. "Please take back the old mare and my mother's anklets. I don't want the bicycle." Returning the pair of scissors to the neighboring shopkeeper, he in his choked voice said to Jagannath Tiwari, "And Uncle, I will also not cut my *choti*."

❖❖❖

6

TWO FACES

When I was studying in M.A. in the subject of Political Science in a college of Meerut, Dal Chand was also in the same college. He did not have a very impressive personality but he was very pleasant to talk to. It is true that he was a great gossip monger but what he mostly said were innocent lies, hyperbolic statements, highly exaggerated accounts of his adventures and achievements, something which people enjoyed though knowing them to be sheer lies and then forgot without carrying any hangover of his words or intentions. His nonsensical and quixotic claims became quotable jokes for a couple of hours – even days.

My first encounter with Dal Chand had taken place in a somewhat dramatic way. As I was moving towards the library, he checked me and said, "Excuse me, Madam, I want to congratulate you. You used to have a dark complexion but now you are as fair as an actress."

Since I did not know the person, I gave a short response in order to get rid of him, "I never had a dark complexion."

"And now you are slim and smart while you were quite bulky earlier."

"I was never bulky."

"Kamini ji, you are changed so much even then you deny everything."

"I am not Kamini but Namita."

"So you have changed your name as well."

Ignoring his comments and without asking his name, I went to join other girls, told them about the encounter I had with the above person and they laughed it away, saying, that the fellow was a mad buffoon named Dal Chand and not much attention was to be paid to what he said or did.

For a number of days, Dal Chand and I had no chance meeting but during the next two years, I with some girls met him many times and listened to his nonsensical and even funny claims and achievements.

After the final examination, my father who was in a nationalised bank in Meerut got transferred to Allahabad. By the end of the year, my parents began to search for a suitable match for me. They were absolutely sure that because of my beauty, none would think of rejecting me.

It turned out to be true. One gentleman named Awadh Raj with his parents came from Benares, saw and selected me. Awadh Raj was working in a bank there. Both of us exchanged our views over our temperaments and interests, liking and disliking. He told me that he had seen me in Meerut, though I had not, because he was studying in a different college. At the time of parting, his father said to my father, "I hope Namita is responsible enough. We have a large family and Awadh Raj is the eldest one who will have to take care of both his younger brother and sister. It cannot be done without the cooperation of his wife."

"Rest assured," my father said. "My daughter Namita too comes from a family of brothers and sisters and knows her duty towards them. After her marriage, she would consider you people as her real parents."

Since I had heard the assurances of my father, I resolved to do everything for Awadh Raj's family. Instead of taking up a job of a teacher, I realised that since my mother-in-law was old and weak, I must help her in every possible way. Besides, I enjoyed the company of my husband and his siblings who together gave the impression of a bubbling happy family.

My husband was quite loving and considerate which made my life exceedingly happy. Within a year of our marriage, I became a mother of one son. Even though my delivery was natural, the physicians recommended blood transfusion because of my weakness. When Awadh Raj informed me of it, I asked him, "Will it be done through intra-venous infusion or... "

"Why Namita? Do you know of some other method?"

I laughed weakly and narrated what Dal Chand had told me in Meerut. Once I and some other girls happened to meet Dal Chand and he had said, "You know, Namita, I have made a machine which can make synthetic blood. It will be so much in demand that in no time, I would be a multi-millionaire. I could also get a Nobel Prize for it. And the best part with this blood is that rather than infusing it through veins, it can easily be taken orally with the same results." The fellow then had shown to all of us a small phial with blood-like substance in it, and had drunk it, though all of us were firmly convinced that it must have been the juice of pomegranate or some coloured liquid.

"Don't talk of Dal Chand," Awadh Raj lightly said. "I know him well because I lived in Meerut for two years in a rented room of his house. He is an idiot of the highest order and should not be taken seriously at all."

My son Shridhar had hardly become six months old when something happened and Awadh Raj began to be unpleasant with me. He had visited Meerut in connection with some official work and on his return he became quite a different person. Since I had studied in Meerut, I suspected that his ears could have been poisoned by someone but I was not sure of it, nor did I ask him the reasons for his changed attitude. Now he always avoided me by remaining preoccupied with his siblings. Even though I liked his helpful attitude to his family, yet with the passage of time, I began to feel occasionally his absence of love for me. Luckily, such a thing did not cause sleepless nights to me because after remaining busy for the whole day, I always fell down dead and had a comfortable, sound sleep in the night.

The loving relationship between my son Shridhar and me kept me happy, otherwise Awadh Raj was becoming more and more angry with me, scolding me over minor slips which could easily have been ignored. I found him perpetually in a mood that if given a choice, he would have liked to thrash me physically. It was not that he was always in a bad mood; I had seen him tickling his younger brother or sister, teasing them, cracking jokes and laughing with them but the moment he saw or came to me, his face became colourless, nearly dark, as if he had donned a different mask for me. Whenever his mother talked about any one's father or mother-in-law, Awadh Raj invariably brought the reference to my parents, showing them all in black colours as if purposely to hurt me. There were times when I felt like giving him a befitting reply, to quarrel with him but the wisdom dawned on me that I must bring up my son well, do my duties to husband and that someday the tide was bound to turn in my favour.

Once in a while, there came times when Awadh Raj appeared to be quite pleasant and happy, and I thought I was going to be blessed in the showers of his ever-spreading pleasantness but the moment he came to me, he was all dark clouds without silver lining, and my expectations were suddenly dashed to the ground. It was on these occasions that I recalled Dal Chand whose conversations and jokes provided momentary relief even after a lapse of a couple of years. One day Awadh Raj, his mother, I and my son Shridhar – all were sitting at the dining table for a cup of tea. Suddenly, Shridhar got up, went up to the fridge, brought out a straw and began to sip tea with it.

"Straws are used, son, normally for cold drinks, not for tea," Awadh Raj advised.

Although his advice was proper, I, remembering something, laughed. It made Awadh Raj angry. Instead of talking directly to me, he asked his mother, "Is there anything funny, mother, in what I said to provoke laughter?"

Envisioning probably the potential seed of a quarrel between us, his mother looked at me and was getting up to go to avoid embarrassment but checking her momentarily and then controlling my laughter, I said, "Mother, I remember, once a class fellow of mine named Dal Chand had picked up in the canteen a straw to sip tea with it and when others had made fun of him, he had said, "My physician has asked me to be as far away from tea as possible." After his mother had left, I became serious and said to him, "How could I dare to laugh at you, Awadh? You are all I have."

My son had become five-year old now. In all these years, Awadh Raj remained the same. As usual, I reconciled to his indifferent even unpleasant attitude, thinking of positive points in the family. His younger brother, sister and even his mother –

all of them were nice to me. There was no further claim of dowry, no beatings, no harassment. Everything else was good. Only his two faces troubled me – one for his siblings and his mother, and the other one for me.

One day, after so many years, his face appeared to be pleasant. I thought, he might be remembering some joke or a pleasant anecdote the way I remember – a sort of passing moment, nothing else, but he came and called me by my name, "Namita."

"Yes," I hurriedly said and ran to him. "What service can I do for you?"

He laughed – a short laugh. It was for the first time after several years that I had seen him coming to me as an husband otherwise he always appeared as a tax collector. I was still looking askance at him, when he softly proposed, "Shall we go for a movie tonight?"

"Movie?" I asked in excitement and disbelief. "Shall we take our son?"

"No. Amma will take care of him. I have asked her." Then after a pause, "We can also take our dinner in a restaurant."

I in my surprise wanted to ask him whether he had got any lottery, prize or promotion to merit this grand opportunity but when I had never questioned him for so many years in the past, I did not say anything, leaving myself as a kite in his hands, moving according to the tugs he gave. Hence I patiently waited for the things to take their own shape.

While sitting in the lobby of the theater, waiting for an entry in the balcony, Awadh Raj said, "Namita, I have been unfair to you for several years. There are many things I wish to talk to you, but before that, let me tell you about Dal Chand. He is in jail."

Somewhat shocked, I wanted to ask him the reason but waited for him to complete the story himself. He resumed, "Do you know, Namita, that he was a trick photographer who could fiddle with all sorts of photos by cutting, transposing, editing and even morphing them?"

"Yes, I know." I said. "His father owned a photo studio and he learnt much of trick photography from him but Dal Chand did it without harming or exploiting anybody. Once he had made my photo with a deer's horns, my face was given to a cow and half of my face was bracketed with a guerrilla-like person like that of Shiva-and-Shakti. He used to do it for fun and I as well as other girls never minded it."

Awadh Raj chuckled and touching my cheek lovingly with his fingers clarified, "Namita that is your mistake. He showed me even your photograph but it was lucky that he did not blackmail you."

"Is that right?" I asked him in an agitated way. "My photos must have been funny ones."

"Not funny ones alone, Namita," he corrected me. "He blackmailed some rich girls by showing them in compromising positions, one of whom complained to the police. It raided his photo studio and found a lot of highly obscene photographs. Let me also disclose that one of the reasons why I was rather unhappy with you was because Dal Chand had shown me, among half-a-dozen shots from college life, your nude photograph lying down on a mattress formed out of the wads of 1000-rupee currency notes. I had visited Meerut with some official work immediately after the birth of our Shridhar. Rather than staying in a hotel, I had stayed for a day with Dal Chand to revive my old memories of my stay in Meerut. He showed me your photos, not knowing that you were married to me. Had he shown them earlier, I would have declined your marriage proposal. It was only a couple of days back that I read the detailed news of his arrest. You know only one of his faces – the pleasant one. Besides, the fact that you casually referred to Dal Chand so frequently in the last many years that had there been any objectionable relationship between you and him, you would have completely avoided referring to him."

When I wiped my tears of gratitude, he quietly pressed my hand in assurance as if to say that everything was fine now.

❖❖❖

7

DISPOSABLE ITEMS

An unemployed youth is a disposable commodity to be tried, used and discarded. At least that is what Deepankar thought. Gifted with a charming personality, fair complexion, sharp features and well-built body, he had a photogenic face which attracted onlookers to him who occasionally suggested, "Why don't you go to Bollywood? You are better looking than many of the movie actors."

He would laugh mutedly, saying, "I would prefer to be a peon in some office to take care of my parents. I don't entertain impractical dreams."

He had done many odd jobs, such as, working at a saw mill where large tree trunks were converted into thick and thin planks totally disposable. Afterwards, he was hired by a kite maker. Deepankar liked the job. Even though the kites he made too were disposable, lasting no more than a few hours but they made him at least momentarily happy as they rose to dizzying heights till someone snapped the thread and they came tumbling down, sinking into oblivion. With the end of the season, he lost his job again.

Concerned at the joblessness of Deepankar, his father took him to a reputed astrologer of the area who was known for the veracity of his predictions. After looking intently at his palms, his horoscope and after making calculations, the astrologer shook his head in the negative, saying, "My son, I am sorry you have no good job in your fate, but there is a good news. You'll have a son who is bound to get a good prestigious job."

His father was a potter and he had no choice but to help him. However, it pained Deepankar that so much of his father's hard labour went into the making of clayey pots and pans which were sold so cheap with many defective ones discarded. His father brought black soil on his mule, soaked it in water, kneaded it first by his feet and then by his hands so that it contained no pebbles at all and then converted it into small lumps of manageable size in order to place them on the potter's wheel.

Deepankar watched with fascinating eyes how the wheel was turned by his father and then by periodically wetting his hands, how these lumps of clay were given different shapes – now a pitcher, now a *surahi* – an earthen jar with a long neck – or a flower vase. Occasionally, his father would philosophize: "Deepankar, I sometimes think that my ancestors remained in this profession for ages, but what have we inherited or what are we going to bequeath to the next generation – virtually nothing other than the potter's wheel and the pieces of broken clayey pots. But if the astrologer's prediction turns out to be true, your son holds a promise for us."

While helping his father, Deepankar thought of one innovation or other in his father's work so that his pots could be different from others. When his father made the *surahi*, the son would engrave something artistically new and fresh with his chisel. The sense of appreciation he got from the customers swelled his heart with pride. That is why occasionally, his father said, "Deepankar, you are lending some momentary identity to our profession – something we had never thought of for generations. It makes me proud of you."

Once an extremely charming lady with sharp-featured face stopped her car by the pile of clayey pots and saw the original engraving on a *surahi* fitted with a faucet. Minutely scrutinising the *surahi,* she exclaimed, "Wonderful! Excellent!" Then looking at the old person, she said, "You have done good work on it."

"No, Madam," he said and pointing out his finger at Deepankar, added, "My son has done it."

She looked at Deepankar's face. As her eyes shone in appreciation, she muttered, "Handsome is who handsomely does." Giving him money, she was about to take it to her car, when Deepankar politely took the *surahi* and placed it in her car.

Appreciating the gesture, she said to Deepankar's father, "Your son is not only unusually handsome but quite well mannered." Turning to Deepankar, she gave him a visiting card and said, "Please visit my office. I am the Manager of a company and would like you to do some occasional work for me for which I would pay you well."

"My pleasure, Madam," Deepankar said, "to be of any service to you."

Thinking a great deal about his father's astrologer-driven dream of making his grandson great in someway, Deepankar could see no way out. His son was now one-year old. Many times thinking of such things, he dreamt that his son had become a Manager of a firm and felt delighted only to be shocked on waking up from his dream.

It was the month of July and clayey pots and pans were nearly out of season except for the poor. It was also not proper occasion for his father to make clayey pots as they got wet and did not dry up for baking. Hence he thought of visiting the lady. Her visiting card read: "Swarna Lata Bansal, Manager, Disposable Items Company."

Even though the name of the company was not very impressive, it was a grand building in which an attendant escorted him to the lady. He was mesmerised by the grandeur of the office with an air conditioner, expensive sofa sets, glass table and impressive shining tapestry. He could not dare to sit when in a sweet voice, Swarna Lata asked him, "Sit down, Deepankar."

She was much more gorgeous, more beautiful than when she had visited his roadside place where his pots were being sold. He felt that with his shabby dress, he appeared to be a dispensable item for some large trash bin.

Swarna Lata picked up the phone and ordered for tea. Deepankar wanted to ask her not to take the trouble but meanwhile she said, "Deepankar, I want you to suggest some clayey pieces for the walls of this room – something innovative. I don't want those common expensive things which are available in the market."

"I'll think about it and tell you later on."

"I'm not yet finished," she continued with a charming smile, and winking her eye. "Deepankar, your father told me that you also know a little about gardening, that you have a small nursery in which you grow flower plants which you sell to the customers. How much does a flower plant cost?"

"Depends on its variety and size of the plant," Deepankar coolly explained. "Those which belong to the common category, I charge around Rs fifteen each whereas those of rarer variety go up to eighty or even one hundred."

"How much money do you earn everyday by selling them – on an average?" When Deepankar remained quiet, she continued, "Say two hundred or so?"

Deepankar waved his head to say yes.

"You come to my residence and I'll show you my little garden on the roof and seek your advice for its improvement."

One evening when Deepankar reached her place, he looked at the flower pots. They were kept in a haphazard manner without any system or pattern. He shifted the positions of some of them. There was one plant of a white rose that was kept far away from others and was wilting. He brought it closer to other rose plants, saying, "The plant was alone. Like human beings, the plants too need each other's company."

"Is that right?" Swarna Lata asked in surprise. "Could this be the reason why a beautiful, multi-colored fish I had put in my aquarium did not eat for two days and died on the third day?"

"Madam, every creature needs company to lead a happy life and to survive whether it is human being, animal or plant. Had you put two or three more of them in the aquarium, it would not have died."

"You seem to be right," Swarna Lata delightfully said. "My husband went abroad about a month back and since I have been alone, people say, that the colour of my face has faded a little."

Deepankar looked at her face and said, "I had not seen you earlier, Madam, and hence I do not know how you looked in the past but now you look exceedingly beautiful and fresh – as fresh as that pink rose in the flower pot."

"Is that right?" Swarna Lata said in excitement. "I feel so happy to hear of it. You are a good boy," she moved forward, caught hold of Deepankar and kissing him on his forehead and both cheeks, said, "You are so handsome and so good."

It was totally unexpected, particularly when he feared being reprimanded for such a comment to a lady far above his social status. In his entire life, he had never touched such a beautiful woman, but this woman was altogether different who kissed him and then asked, "I hope you did not mind it. I feel free with a person I like."

Deepankar felt happy because at the back of his mind, he had the prediction of the astrologer about his son getting a prestigious job. His acquaintance with the lady raised his hopes for his son's future.

Swarna Lata persuaded him to live in her house for a month or two so that she would not feel lonely or else she might fall ill. When he agreed, she got some tolerably decent clothes purchased for him. Occasionally he used her husband's clothes which fitted him well. When Deepankar's wife and parents complained about his absence from home, he consoled them that it was only for two months and in any case, he was visiting his house for a couple of hours on Sundays. He told them that so much money from any other source was unthinkable. His one month's income was more than the income from selling clayey pots and flower plants for the entire year. The best part was that the money thus saved could be used for his son's education which was needed for the fulfillment of the astrologer's prediction.

After two months, Swarna Lata told him that his services were no longer needed as her husband was coming back. Deepankar asked her, "Can't you give me a job in your company?"

"No, Deepankar. I am sorry," Swarna Lata said. "It wouldn't be desirable because many people of the company have seen us together and I don't want tales to be bandied about close to scandals."

When his son Jyotirmaya became five-year old, Deepankar got him admitted to a standard English medium school of Meerut city. When he reached the fifth standard, he told Deepankar, "Father, I have been hearing for a number of days that there was another boy who had a similar face as mine. Today I saw him face to face and it appeared as if I were looking at my own self. How is it possible, Father?"

Initially he remained quiet and then said after a pause, "It is quite possible though rather uncommon."

Deepankar was nearly 45 now. His son Jyotirmaya had done a Master's degree in Political Science. Naturally now a father's desire was to see Jyotirmaya settled in a job. It is not that he had much faith in the prediction about his son's future of getting a prestigious job, but he could not totally dismiss the idea. He knew that one could get a reasonably good job only when he begins it at the lower end. It is like the bottom of the staircase through which one could reach higher, possibly to the top.

Remembering his old association with Swarna Lata, Deepankar thought that she could not do anything for him because of the fear of scandals, but she certainly could fix Jyotirmaya in her company. Accompanied by his son and his Curriculum Vitae in hand, Deepankar went to the Manager's Office of the Disposable Items Company. As they sat down, a gentleman in the chair asked Deepankar, "Yes, gentleman what can I do for you?"

Looking at the face of the Manager very intently, Deepankar was so much lost that he did not hear a word of what the former had said.

"Hello!" the Manager drew Deepankar's attention, somewhat louder now. "You are lost somewhere. Can I do anything for you?"

"Sorry sir," Deepankar apologised. "I wanted to see Madam Swarna Lata."

Somewhat surprised, the Manager asked, "How do you happen to know my mother?"

Showing the visiting card Swarna Lata had given him, he said, "Once she had promised to help me" and handing over the CV, he added, "This is my son's CV."

The Manager looked at a glance at the CV and said, "Right now there is no vacancy in the company. Whenever there is any vacancy, I will get in touch with you."

The indication was that Deepankar and his son must leave, but before going, he asked the Manager, "Where is Madam? I have not seen her for many years."

The Manager said, "She is no more. My father and mother both died in a car accident, but before that they had made me the Manager."

"So sorry to hear of it," he said. "She was a great lady."

The Manager looked again at Jyotirmaya and remained quite surprised in finding his own image identical with that of the applicant. As a matter of fact, they appeared to be twins. Unable to suppress his curiosity, he casually asked Deepankar, "Did your wife work at any time at my father's house?"

"No, never," Deepankar emphatically said, "but I worked for Madam Swarna Lala when she was alone and your father had gone abroad."

The meeting ended abruptly and Deepankar came back disappointed. He pondered deeply over the whole thing and chuckled at the way in which God chose to fulfill the astrologer's prediction!

❖❖❖

8

DIFFERENT FROM OTHERS

Each time Vinay Kumar encountered eunuchs, something strange happened within him. It was the feeling not exactly of hate, but some sort of irritation, a certain undefined uneasiness, the kind one has on finding an ungratefully shameless guest pressing your door bell when you are reluctant to let him in. Since his pre-adolescent years, he had seen them in so many activities of shameless extortions none of which could be justified socially, economically or morally.

It was the occasion of the birth of one of Vinay Kumar's several younger brothers in his town when he found four odd-shaped, dark coloured, gaudily-dressed eunuchs clapping and dancing with merely a *dholak* – a drum. Even when he did not have much of a discriminating faculty as far as music and dance were concerned, he was filled with a feeling of distaste when they shamelessly took his father in their midst, nearly forcing him to accompany them in their dancc much to the delight of the children and even of adults all around, though totally embarrassing his sober-tempered father.

The eunuchs demanded a huge sum of money, which was nearly four times his father's monthly salary as a Patwari and in any case which he used to give in toto to his eldest brother. When they found that no money was coming to them, one by one three of them made gestures of making love to him – one encircling his neck with a hand, the second one caressing his head and tweaking his cheeks and the third one encircling his waist and advancing in dancing steps. His father's discomfort was quite visible on his face which seemed close to tears. In his pathetic state, he called his son, "Vinay, go and call your eldest *bua* as I have no money at all."

Going inside the house, Vinay Kumar brought his *bua* – his father's sister – who was in charge of all the household expenses. Seeing the embarrassment of her brother, she gave the eunuchs some money which they refused to accept, demanding more and more.

"This is not the birth of the first son but that of the seventh one," she clarified. "It is no more a matter of jubilation. Hence the amount I am giving is good enough."

"In that case, we'll take the father of the newly born son with us," their leader threatened, "and convert him to be a member of our society." It was clear that the eunuch was threatening to make her brother a eunuch by castrating him.

Giving a little more money, his *bua* held her brother's hand and pulled him away from amongst them.

Though the incident had produced a lot of fun and laughter to the onlookers, it produced in Vinay Kumar an abhorrent feeling of a forced sense of injustice inflicted on the family without any logical reason. It anguished him that the eunuchs had made a mockery of his father with whom he silently sympathised. On that day, the first impression created by the eunuchs was imprinted on his memory like an invisible injury.

❖❖❖

Even though Monika was born and brought up as a small, fair-complexioned girl in a middle class Rajput family in Haryana and was exceedingly beautiful, for inexplicable reasons she was not allowed to play outside with others. While her father never liked or even spoke to her, her mother's love remained the sole surviving straw to save her from sinking in gloom and despondency. Whenever Monika cried or protested to her mother why she was not being allowed to play outside like her other brothers or sisters, her mother simply said, "Monika, I am afraid if I let you go outside, some eunuchs will whisk you away, never to let you visit our home again."

The girl did not know then what the word eunuchs meant but she imagined them to be a group of horrible-looking people who kidnapped beautiful girls, never allowing them to go back home. She failed to understand why should she alone, of all the children, be whisked away by the eunuchs? On her insistence, her mother simply explained that she was not being allowed because she was a *hijari* – a eunuch.

"What is a eunuch?" Monika asked. "How am I a eunuch?"

With a great difficulty, she said, "Because you are different from others."

Unable to suppress her anger, Monika asked, "How different? Do I have four legs or two horns or one tail? What makes me different from others?" and she began to give heart-rending, loud cries.

Her mother with great difficulty checked her own tears and clasping the girl to her heart said in her choked voice, "I have no heart to explain it, Monika. If I had a choice, I would keep you well-protected inside my heart."

She went to her grandmother whom Monika loved the most. Seeing the poor girl crying inconsolably, the grandmother felt pity and embraced her warmly. She showed the girl and then explained to her how the latter was different from others, particularly from both brothers and sisters. Now rather than blaming her parents, Monika began to blame god; it was He who was the real culprit. It was He who had made her different from others.

When her other brothers and sisters began to go to school, Monika insisted on going with them. First of all her mother refused to let her go out but on the girl's heart-rending cries, she allowed her to do so. Her mother's objection was: "If a eunuch comes to know about you, she'll snatch you away from us."

In the school, Monika was very happy because none knew that she was different from them. Her beautiful face came to her rescue. However, the moment she entered the house, it seemed a prison for her because it was there that she was denied a rightful place and was treated as an untouchable. When her father came, her brothers and sisters went and sat in his lap, or played with him, but he had strictly forbidden her mother from allowing Monika to go even before his eyes, or else he would kill her by striking her head against a stone slab. It was obvious he did not want to see her face. He boasted, it was his generosity that he was letting the girl stay in the family; otherwise, to have a eunuch is an unbearable humiliation to the Rajput who earlier used to sacrifice the daughters' lives in order to keep their heads proudly high.

As Monika grew to be a teenager, her face became more captivating. When she had reached the tenth class, some boys began to look at her amorously. It made her feel happy. Suffering from inferiority complex and absence of father's love, the mere appreciative glances of the ogling boys sprouted some seeds of love and confidence within her, though she restrained herself from jumping into their embraces.

In High School examination, she secured the highest marks among all the students in school, surpassing the percentage of her elder brothers and sisters. When her mother cheerfully hugged and kissed the daughter, praising her for her hard work, Monika mischievously asked, "Am I not different from others, Mother?"

There was no scope for further education in the town of Bhadura where they lived and Monika began to stay at home, occasionally moving out for stray grocery items or for fresh vegetables. One day, a boy quietly followed her. She was conscious of it, but she ignored him and disappeared into her house. After a week, he followed her again. Monika asked him, "Why do you follow me?"

"I like you and want to talk to you. Would you mind if I invite you for a cup of tea in a nearby restaurant?"

She hesitated and then agreed to accompany him. He began, "My name is Shiv Lal. You are so beautiful. What is your name?"

Keeping quiet for sometime, she looked at his face and then told him, "My name is Monika but I am not what you think of me, Shiv Lal. You'll be disappointed when I tell you who am I!"

"For me you are the most beautiful creature on earth, Monika, and it does not matter who you are!" Shiv Lal said grandly in all happiness.

Monika laughed a little and he seemed to like her laughter but when she said, "I am a *kinnar* or *hijari* – a eunuch." His face fell as if he had accidentally tasted a bitter pill when he was expecting a sweet one. The cup of tea he had in his hand had nearly fallen. Shiv Lal did not follow her afterwards; obviously, he must have been disappointed.

After a couple of days, Shiv Lal rang her up and wanted to meet her. They met again in the same restaurant. He said, "Monika, I realised during the last one week that I cannot live without you and would like to marry you."

Monika laughed so loudly that other persons in the restaurant began to look at them. Then slowly she said, "You know I am incapable of giving you any child."

"I know it and I have thought about it," Shiv Lal said. "We can always adopt one."

After their marriage, they lived well for a couple of months. She had already left her home for good. Monika did not know that Shiv Lal was a criminal and that a case was continuing in a court of law against him. When the judgment came, he was awarded eight years' jail. She stayed alone for sometime and then one day she was spotted by a group of eunuchs which she joined.

❖❖❖

One day Vinay Kumar was traveling with his niece Shikha – his sister's daughter – from New Delhi to Gwalior in an express train. At Agra Cantt railway station, some eunuchs forcibly boarded the compartment. Even though it was a reserved 3-tier compartment, they entered it without any hesitation as if the train belonged to them. They were in a group of four who shamelessly began to collect money from each of the passengers. The method of their collection was so crude, so much devoid of human sensibility, so shameless that one more layer of hatred against them was added in his heart. He knew that they were poor, that none gave them jobs, but that did not justify their act of collecting money by throttling all human considerations.

That is why, the mere sight of these creatures usually aroused feelings within him that they were a burden on the society, on the sensitivities of the people. Why couldn't they do some work? There were thousands of things they could do – become hawkers or petty shopkeepers or rickshawallahs and so on. But why do anything when you can get a lot of money simply by extortion! Some people may argue that it was not extortion but begging; but begging for alms demands humility whereas they arrogantly shamed the donors. On the auspicious occasions of the birth of a child, in marriage functions, or in house warming ceremonies, they demanded so much of money that the amount went into thousands of rupees! It was a sort of daytime loot! Vinay Kumar saw in the compartment that when any passenger pathetically but politely declined to give any money, explaining his difficulties, they humiliated the person so much that he had no choice but to empty his pocket. When a T.T.E. came in the compartment and demanded tickets from them, they harassed him so much that the fellow not only remained helpless but had to give some money to them. The eunuchs demanded money from Vinay Kumar, too, and he had to give them some amount, but in anger he and his niece Shikha misbehaved with them. Suspecting later on that he might have hurt their feelings, Vinay Kumar looked at their faces; he found no traces of any adverse effect on them and they were as chirpy as ever.

His seven-year old niece Shikha was gleefully playing with other children, climbing on upper berths, getting down, even jumping here and there. Suddenly there was a sharp cry from her. Vinay Kumar ran to her and found there was a deep two-inch cut on her forehead from which blood was coming out profusely. One of the eunuchs hurried to her, tore a part of her saree, tied the wound and placing the girl in her lap, kept the wound pressed with her hand. He found that the eunuch's saree was blood-stained. Vinay Kumar told her apologetically, "I am sorry your saree has been spoiled."

"Don't worry, sir, about the saree," she said. "The child is worth many such sarees in the world. Our car is coming at the Gwalior station to receive us. First of all we'll have the girl admitted to hospital to have a proper diagnosis and treatment. The girl comes first. We'll go home later."

When they reached the Gwalior station, I and Shikha were taken in the Maruti Omni to a hospital. One eunuch who had come to receive them was Monika who was exceedingly beautiful and sweet to talk to. In the hospital, the surgeon declared that the patient needed immediate blood transfusion but her blood group was O-negative which is considered uncommon and was not available in the hospital. Since Vinay Kumar's own blood group too did not match with that of his niece, he was extremely worried. Meanwhile, to his surprise, Monika declared that she had the same uncommon blood group – O-negative – and would be glad to donate it for the cause of the girl. It was her blood that was given to Shikha.

The activities and attitudes of these eunuchs were altogether contrary to Vinay Kumar's lifelong impressions, prejudices and conclusions. On deep contemplation, he realised that the eunuchs had shown much more consideration and humanity for his injured niece than he himself could have done for anybody else.

When Shikha became fully recovered, Vinay Kumar went with her to Monika's place to express his profound gratitude. He was surprised to find her house neat and clean. Everything in the drawing room was properly arranged. A daily newspaper was kept on the centre table. Vinay Kumar began, "Monika, we are grateful for what you people did for my niece on that day."

"It was our duty, sir. After all we too are human beings."

After discussing other things, Vinay Kumar humbly said, "Monika, if you don't mind, I would like to ask you a question very frankly. All my life I had nothing but unpleasant experiences of encountering eunuchs at several places, but you are so diametrically opposite to them. What could be the reason?"

Giving a broad smile, Monika said, "Sir, one gives what one has or receives. The world treats the eunuchs so badly that they have not known what good treatment is. I was among the luckiest ones who for various reasons was treated relatively well, though I am no less sore for being ill-treated by my father. But in life, I got love, friendship and respect which I try to give to others."

"Has your family reconciled to your present situation?"

She kept quiet but tears began to well up in her eyes and after wiping them off, she said, "Unfortunately no. After being elected as a ward representative of the Gwalior Municipal Corporation, I went to my home in all happiness to disclose this news to my mother, thinking that it would make her very happy and proud of me, but she exploded in an unexpectedly harsh tone, saying, 'How dare you come to my house? This house is closed for you forever. Turn your face and go.' After that I never tried to go there. It pains me that I could never in my life talk to my father."

Vinay Kumar apologetically said, "I am sorry, Monika, I have scratched your hidden wound, but it is surprising that you don't show your anger in your attitude or behaviour."

By this time, she had composed herself completely and said, "It is because of my behaviour that I am an elected representative of a ward. They are pressing hard that I contest for the post of Mayor. But it is too early for that."

"Is that the reason why you are living separately whereas most eunuchs tend to stay together?"

"That is true, sir," Monika smiled. "I am the only eunuch who is educated and I cherish a mission in life. My plan is to make the eunuchs behave well with the public and in return to secure a respectable place for the third gender legally and socially. By doing so I'll prove in a better way what my mother had derogatively told me in my childhood that I am different from others."

❖❖❖

9

A TEACHER OF HUMANITY

Dr Mohinder Singh was a dentist. To visit him was to take a lesson in humanity and human relationships. His small two-room dental clinic was in the heart of the Shastri Market on way to the Golden Temple in Amritsar. It was a highly congested area in which even two-wheelers wriggled out of the traffic with difficulties, turning right and left, requesting a lady here or warning an old man there to give him a passage. No four wheelers were allowed to operate there.

Since Dr Mohinder Singh charged a very low amount of fee for all dental problems – root canal treatment, filling of cavities, fixing of crowns on broken or partially damaged teeth or even in preparing dentures for old men and women – his clinic always remained crowded by patients of middle and lower classes.

In the centre of the room, there was the patient's chair with all paraphernalia while in one corner of the clinic, his son-in-law Sohan Singh worked on fixing and filing teeth embedded in one mould or other so that the dentures fit in comfortably in the mouths of his old toothless patients. It was a very long procedure which was done meticulously by Sohan Singh under the supervision of Dr Mohinder Singh. He had a small motor with several small attachable files for rubbing away the superfluous material and a candle with which he fixed the artificial teeth in the moulds of dentures. Occasionally, he was asked to help the dentist in extracting a decayed tooth whose roots were so deep that the old dentist found it difficult to uproot as if it were a well-rooted stump of an otherwise skeletal tree.

Dr Mohinder Singh was a well-dressed man often in a pair of pants and half shirt, a turban over his head and steel-rimmed eye glasses which together lent a shade of attraction to his fair-complexioned personality. Unlike other Sikh gentlemen of the Punjab who were healthy and large-sized, he looked to be very slim. Even though his moustache and beard were white, they were well-glued so that they obediently remained fixed to the place where they were ordered to be in the morning.

The dentist called each patient one by one but without assigning any token number or writing their names in a register. Rather than completing the work of one patient fully and then freeing him, he would do a little work on a couple of patients one by one and then ask them to wait in the next room or outside, making each one feel comfortable with a feeling that they were being cared for simultaneously and that they would not have to wait for a long time for their treatment. The dentist's casual talk with each patient made him feel at home that his antecedents were known to the dentist and this personal touch reassured him that a good care would be taken of his teeth.

I was working in the University of Amritsar. Since I was from Patna in Bihar, Dr Mohinder Singh would particularly feel more warm towards me, god knows why. I had many tooth-related problems, such as, cavities and root-canal treatments. For filling the cavity of a tooth, he would drill my infected tooth, clean it well, and then place Betadine-soaked tiny piece of cotton swab into it and then would let me wait outside. Many times for filling purpose, he would place some silvery powder stuff in a tiny glass mortar, asking me to grind it very slowly with a very small pestle and then he would place it in the cavity of my tooth. When the question of making payment finally came, I would ask him, "How much to pay to you?"

In response, he would simply fold both of his hands and say, "Nothing. I am obliged you came to my clinic."

The question was repeatedly asked by me but each time he folded his hands and finally told me, "It is an honour to be of any service to a learned man like you."

Without asking further questions, I would place a certain reasonable amount in his hands and come back to my residence after practically learning a lesson in courtesy, generosity and humanity.

❖❖❖

The incidents of terrorism in Punjab were increasing day by day in the early 1980's. There was an undercurrent of fear all around which no one articulated in words or behaviour but one could read it on their faces. The atmosphere was such that when someone went out of station within the Punjab, the people were not sure of their survival and safe return till they actually came back home.

My parents and relations asked me to come back home in Bihar, leaving Punjab as the violent conditions kept everyone on thorns and brambles. Thc newspapers carried long stories of Hindus being killed at all the places in the Punjab. First of all the terrorists targeted rickshaw-wallahs and petty kiosk owners selling betel leaves and pouches of tobacco who formed a good number in cities and hailed from Bihar, Madhya Pradesh and Uttar Pradesh. Afterwards, they targeted the rich and influential Hindus from Punjab itself so that their assets may be taken over after their elimination as also to demoralise the rest of the

Hindus. To come even to the dentist's clinic was not easy, though the good part was that he was a very gentle Sikh person who paid great respect to me. Even otherwise, the days were safer than nights and due to it, I voluntarily observed dusk-to-dawn curfew hours for a number of years.

When the hardcore terrorists had taken shelter in the basement of the Golden Temple, even a visit to it was not considered safe. There were rumours that even those Sikh young men who got recently married and went to pay their obeisance to the temple, and if their wives happened to be beautiful, they alone were held back for the "blessings" which was a sort of code word for kidnapping within the temple itself. The husbands were given stern threats of the elimination of their entire families in case they reported the matter to the police or law-enforcement agencies which made them seal their lips against the incidents. Though I did not believe in such rumours, people continued to relish them, adding salt and pepper to make them quite juicy. Such stories were repeated among the people of all religions, making them naturally quite nervous.

Amid all this violence, the dentist's clinic was an island of peace and humanity. Dr Singh treated each patient with kindness and affability as if each one were an ambassador from God coming on this earth with assigned duties. It was with me that he particularly discussed many things and even when he was treating others, he would make me sit on a stool in a corner of the working room in order to talk with me.

One day when other patients were outside, I casually asked him, "Doctor Sahib, I have a simple question. You are uniformly good and behave well with all your patients, but you are extra kind and considerate to me. Why this special favour?"

Dr Mohinder Singh smiled, continued to think, then came to me and placing both of his hands on my shoulders, slowly whispered, "Most of my patients are from poor families and are not even literate with whom one can discuss the country's affairs. You are educated and intelligent, teaching in the university, have come from abroad and above all you see things in their totality and hence talking with you is not only a matter of pleasure but enlightening in certain ways."

He went out, talked to all patients whom he knew personally and then called one of them inside to be in the patient's chair. I thought over all his words, wondering whether it was an exaggerated account of me or it had an expression of his genuine feelings and the latter appeared to be true. Whenever I sat outside, I looked at the clothes of his patients, tracked their conversation and found that most people talked about their miserable ways of living, occasionally accompanied by their half-naked children. Dr Mohinder Singh treated them with the same attention and care as he would me.

A patient was sitting on the dentist's chair with a slightly swollen face. Dr Mohinder asked him, "What is the problem?"

"A tooth is giving me unbearable pain."

"Which tooth?"

"You go to the balcony and then the last seat in the last row – I mean the last tooth – on the right hand side."

Dr Mohinder Singh smiled and asked him, "Do you work in some movie theatre?"

"Yes, but how do you know sir?" the patient asked in surprise.

Dr Mohinder might have understood, as I had, by the way he had described the location of the troublesome tooth, but he said nothing; instead, he smilingly asked, "In which theatre do you work?"

"Krishna Theatre," he said in excitement. "Please come to see any movie sir. I'll arrange a free pass for you."

While sitting in the clinic, many poor patients were treated who had no money to pay his fees, Dr Singh not only gave them full attention but did not charge anything from them. In addition, he gave them medicines free of charge. Seeing his attitude towards the poor, I said, "Sir, I know of many physicians and even dentists who charge exorbitant fees from the poor and yet none treats them with so much consideration as you do."

Stopping the drilling work, he cleaned the patient's cavity with a thin jet of water from a syringe, gave a Betadine-soaked tiny cotton swab and then said, "If God has made me capable of doing something, I feel blessed and do so accordingly. I am an old person, capable of doing nothing else. I feel happy in doing this little bit for the poor in the name of humanity. I really feel pleasure in doing so."

❖❖❖

After a couple of visits to the dentist, we felt somewhat close to each other. He had already introduced his son-in-law Sohan Singh to me. When he was not in the clinic, Dr Mohinder Singh told me a few more things about his family. He said that he has a beautiful daughter Preeti, who is exceedingly beautiful.

"I can imagine her from your handsome face."

"No, you cannot, as she is far more beautiful. You come to our residence on the next Sunday. I would like you to meet and talk to her a little about simple sentences of spoken English but remember she is totally blind."

"Blind?" I was shocked.

"Yes, since birth," he said.

"But she is married. Isn't Sohan Singh your son-in-law? How did he marry her?"

Smiling, he comforted me by placing his hands on my shoulders and said, "Randeep Lal, the world has both good people and bad people. I found an honest orphan, that is, Sohan Singh, who willingly became prepared to marry her and to stay on with us after marriage. This arrangement keeps all of us happy."

On Sundays, I began to visit Dr Mohinder Singh's residence and made his daughter learn a few simple sentences in English. She felt visibly happy in learning them and internalised them.

As we were sitting, a small beautiful child came with a small bottle, asking the dentist, "Badde Papaji, please put this oil in my head."

"No my dear son," he said, taking away the bottle of hair-fixer from him. "This is not good for you."

"When you can use it, Badde Papa, why can't I?" the boy questioned.

Kissing him, he said, "It turns one's hair white."

"Oh, that is why you have white hair."

After Preeti too had gone inside, Dr Mohinder Singh sat very close to me and said, "The boy Sohan Singh is very poor and has none else in the world. By marrying my daughter and staying on with us, he has a family, Prreti has a husband and a child as well as her parents!"

"Wonderful arrangement," I said and then after a pause, "How is Sohan Singh?"

"Extremely gentle and religious-minded. Though Preeti is blind, he takes her to the Golden Temple happily every now and then. We are very happy with each other. Now my son who is abroad is to be married off. I hope we get a good bride."

❖❖❖

One day Dr Mohinder Singh came quite late and appeared somewhat worried. He observed the usual courtesies but the ever-present cheerfulness was missing from his face. As his habit was, he asked each patient what the problem was and if some patients told of complicated cases which demanded too much of time, he folded his hands courteously and asked them to come later as he was to go home soon.

When I too asked his permission to leave, he hinted at me to stay on. After taking care of two patients who needed urgent attention, he called me. I wanted to have a cavity of my tooth cleaned and filled in. When I sat on the dentist's chair, I asked him, "Doctor Sahib, what makes you so worried? You may tell me if it is not too confidential."

He kept quiet and murmured, "There is nothing so confidential that I cannot share with you."

"You were quite busy in arranging your son's wedding. Everything was done in an excellent manner. Now you should be happy and take a week's holiday. I saw in the wedding ceremony that your daughter-in-law is exceedingly beautiful. Please don't mind if I say that she is as beautiful as any Bollywood actress."

One does not know what happened but suddenly there were tears in his eyes, and before I could ask him anything, he went to a corner of the clinic. I could see his body jerking convulsively as if some invisible force were shaking him. Then wiping off his tears, he folded his hands, requesting me to go away.

I came back home but it troubled me to see what could have been the reason for the tears of this stoic person whose cheerfulness had become an inseparable part of his personality. A Sikh gentleman who was very close to Dr Mohinder Singh and through whom I had begun to know the dentist was diplomatically quiet about it. When I probed with insistence, he said, "Do you promise that you won't tell anyone about it?" After I had assured him of not leaking out anything, he confided, "You were in the marriage of his son and had seen how beautiful his daughter-in-law is. His son along with his newly-wedded wife went to the Golden Temple to seek the blessings but some terrorists, finding his daughter-in-law exceedingly beautiful, whisked her away. Taking the husband in a corner, a gun-toting terrorist told him in clear words the unwritten law that he was to file no complaint to the police station and to say nothing to others or else the entire family would have to bear the consequences.

What had happened was not unusual but something always feared. After sending his son back to the U.S. for his safety, Dr Mohinder Singh moved quietly from place to place even though most well-meaning people advised, even warned him that his efforts were futile and the more he talked about it, the more problems would have to be confronted by him not only in terms of the loss of his reputation but also from revengeful terrorists.

I continued teaching English once a week to his daughter, though occasionally I failed to come for several reasons. His blind daughter told me that Dr Mohinder Singh was so much upset that many times he would walk up and down for hours in the night.

"Did you see it yourself?" I casually asked.

She smiled and then said, "I wish I could see, but I am familiar with his footsteps."

"I am sorry, but this is what I meant."

"It's all right," Preeti kept quiet, staring as if she were looking at some particular place and then added, "It is painful to hear him pacing up and down. Many times just in the middle of night whenever any sound of footstep is heard in the street or near the door, he just opens it to see if his daughter-in-law had come!"

I had to go to Patna in summer vacation. After a month when I came back to Amritsar, I went to Dr Mohinder Singh's residence to see the dentist as well as to teach his daughter. When I pressed the call bell, I confronted a man I had not seen in the past. He was a clean-shaven man without a beard and a turban. Probably he was Dr Mohinder Singh's brother, because the facial features, height and complexion – they were similar to those of the dentist.

After taking a seat, I asked him, "Has Doctor Sahib gone somewhere? I am Randeep Lal who taught his daughter Preeti on Sundays. I never met you before, sir. You must be Doctor Mohinder Singh's brother, though he never told me about you."

He smiled and said, "I am your Doctor Sahib."

It was a stunning moment. Had he declared that he had become a terrorist, I would not have been shocked as much as I was on seeing him clean-shaven, short-haired, turban-less person. Refusing to believe his words, dumb-founded initially, I thought that his brother – younger or elder – was trying to fool me. Since I knew the dentist so well, he was not going to succeed in confusing me. Hence I said, "Though I have never met you before, sir, you have the same voice, the same height and the same facial features as those of the doctor. Where has he gone?"

Hugging me warmly and addressing me by name, he said, "Randeep Lal, it is I, Dr Mohinder Singh, in a new incarnation. As we had discussed in the past, religion without humanity is merely an exhibition of external features – like a cover on any book – a cap, a tilak or a turban. What is happening in the holiest of our shrines? My newly married daughter-in-law was kidnapped inside the shrine! My attempts to trace her resulted in several threats to my family night and day. Since I ignored their threats, they whisked away your blind student Preeti too when she was visiting the temple with Sohan Singh, while the high priests of the religion say nothing. In my helplessness in this old age, I can do nothing but penalise myself. I cannot commit suicide because so many people depend on me but I can renounce the religion which has been a part of our ancestry."

Saying this and hugging me again, he cried like a child, and then mumbled, "You can't understand Randeep Lal, how painful it is to abandon something which has been with us for generations, but that is the way of my simple protest, since I can do nothing else against the powerful institution."

As I was leaving with leaded steps in my own helplessness, his wife and Sohan Singh begged me not to leave the dentist alone but to visit him more frequently as the latter was quite upset and might do something unexpected. Realising his pathetic condition and keeping in mind his kindness and affability towards me all along in the past, I began to visit his house as usual on Sundays, now not to teach his blind daughter Preeti, as she was no longer there, but to take Dr Mohinder Singh out of Amritsar in visiting various places.

Both of us would go to some place or other in Punjab in order to change his mood. With him, I too enjoyed seeing various places in the state which I had not seen earlier. We would take a passenger train or a bus to nearby places so that we could come back to Amritsar in the evening, such as, Batala, Gurdaspur, Pathankot, Khadoor Sahib, Beas, Phagwara, Wagha Border and many other places. Such visits did bring a change in the dentist and he began to forget the tragedies of kidnappings of his daughter and his daughter-in-law. He even occasionally cracked jokes which made me feel very happy that in certain ways, I was paying him back in driblets what he had given to me in bucketfuls. One day he proposed that we go to Taran Taran – a historical place – which has a grand Gurudwara. I expressed my hesitation because it was one place which was known to be haunted by terrorists, but he said they operated in the night and therefore there was no fear during daytime.

After enjoying our visit to Taran Taran including its grand Gurudwara, a little before sunset, we caught a passenger train to Amritsar. It was quite crowded as most people were returning to their homes. When it was just one station away from Amritsar, there were ominous sounds of shots being fired. We heard the pathetic cries and wailings of passengers from other compartments. Before I could understand what was happening, Dr Mohinder Singh asked me to lie down under the wooden long seat of the compartment and nearly shoved me below it. Then he also lay down the same way, covering me by his frail body. Since it was dusk, we dreaded with our palpitating hearts what was to happen. I proposed to him to let him go inside whereas I would cover him from outside, but he insisted that since he was a Sikh, there was a chance of his being saved, but being a Hindu I would definitely be shot.

For a moment, I wanted to tell him that he did not have the visible symbols of Sikhism and might be misunderstood as a Hindu but there was no time for discussion as he placed his hand on my mouth, asking me to be quiet. Within a few seconds, many more people lay down under the long passenger seats, but all of them could not have done so. Meanwhile, two gun-wielding, masked men came and blindly shot those passengers sitting or lying down who had no beards or turbans. There were yells and cries all around. Then the terrorists disappeared in the dark. Before leaving the place, they ordered the driver to take the train to Amritsar.

After the train had begun to move, I called Dr Mohinder Singh again and again, first slowly, then loudly, shook his body vigorously but there was no response. I pulled him out from below the wooden seat but found him all silent. Even though his body was bleeding profusely, I shook his head again, sprinkled drops of water on his face, sought the help of other passengers but they all said that he was senseless. As soon as the train reached Amritsar, I took him to a nearby hospital but the physicians declared him dead on arrival.

The next day, the newspapers reported the deaths of thirty five Hindus in the shootings in the Taran Taran passenger train. I sat gloomily having a terribly miserable feeling at home with a sense of realisation that I had lost a great teacher of humanity.

❖❖❖

10

OF FAR AND NEAR

Distances have always puzzled Kirti Prakash and many times he failed to grasp the meanings of far and near whether they were physical distances or those among friends and relations. From his childhood, he had been told by his parents as to who were his closest relations and who the distant ones – the implication being that all sorts of help was to be expected only from the former.

Jamuna Das and Safdar Khan were neighbours who lived on the outskirts of Lucknow. Disregarding different religions, their families lived in a very friendly way, mixing freely, participating in each other's festivals, joys and sorrows. Even though Kirti Prakash was Jamuna Das's only son, he spent most of his time in the house of Safdar Khan. Being a retired police constable, Safdar Khan always stayed at home and played all sorts of games with both Kirti, aged five, and his own son Naushad, aged seven. Both the children studied in the same school, played together and were happy in each other's company. Jamuna Das and Safdar Khan felt gratified that their friendship had gone to the second generation.

Once Safdar Khan, Naushad and Kirti Prakash visited a neighbouring village in a marriage party. The house was on a small hillock, not very far from their village. In the evening, Naushad had strayed somewhere with his friends whereas Kirti was with him. Safdar Khan began to do some child-talk, asking him, "Kirti, do you see that moon? Is it the same moon we had in our village or some other one?"

"Must be a different one," Kirti said innocently, "because the moon of our village fell down into our well and got drowned. Both Naushad and I saw it in the well before coming here."

Safdar Khan laughed and said, "No, Kirti. No. It is the same moon. You must have seen its reflection in the well. By the way, can you see our village from here?"

"No, it is very far."

"Tell me, Kirti, between our village and the moon, which one is farther?"

"The village is farther and the moon is nearer because I can see the moon and not the village."

Safdar Khan laughed and then explained, "Kirti, what looks close may not always be so. The moon that you see is very very far – miles and miles away and is very large but from the distance it looks very small and quite close to us. In life distances could be deceptive. What or who looks distant may be close and also the other way round."

Kirti Prakash failed to understand what Safdar Khan was professing and he asked, "Chacha Jaan, is it true that there is an old lady in the moon who makes yarn on the spinning wheel?"

"Yes, Kirti," Safdar Khan laughed. "The kurta I am wearing is made of the same yarn spun by the lady in the moon."

"Is it really true, Chacha Jaan?" Kirti asked.

"No, my son Kirti," Safdar Khan said, kissing him. "I was just teasing you as you often tease me."

When Kirti was in High School, his father Jamuna Das died in an accident. Since he had landed property, his wife with the help of Kirti managed the agriculture and the household affairs. Safdar Khan not only gave the family moral support but also good advice in the hour of their need. Safdar Khan's wife Aamna was a beautiful lady who was very friendly with Kirti and his mother. Her company became a source of great strength to them, particularly after Jamuna Das's death.

There were times when a swing was slung from a thick branch of the *neem* tree in the courtyard of Safdar Khan on which turn by turn Naushad and Kirti took rides. They competed in taking its wooden bar to various heights by pushing it with vigorous jerks of their feet but in which Naushad always excelled. Once Kirti felt that he had taken the swing higher than that of Naushad but Safdar Khan judged that his son's swing bar had gone higher than that of Kirti. The latter remained silent and came back home somewhat disappointed. Unable to reconcile himself to it, he narrated the incident to his mother and then added, "I feel that Chacha Jaan always favours Naushad. Why?"

His mother kissed him and laughingly said, "Because Naushad is his own blood; you are a distant one, belonging to different parents of a different religion."

As the time progressed, Safdar Khan's wife died of prolonged illness, Naushad got married, had two children and his business also flourished. To him, the house they were living in began to appear rather small and fairly old fashioned but which Safdar Khan did not want to leave because of his nostalgic attachment to it. On the contrary, Naushad and his wife were getting fast disenchanted with the house and its surroundings. The ways and manners of Safdar Khan had begun to irritate his daughter-in-law and she all the time complained to her husband Naushad how his father went on coughing and spitting in the pot all the time, how he sat on the sofa cross-legged as though he were in a country feast or squatted on it with both his feet well planted as if he were in a country-type toilet, and how his clothes emitted a foul smell. Besides, his way of sipping tea from a plate with slurping sounds or of taking meals noisily with dog-like movement of jaws appeared nauseating. Even though Naushad knew that some of her charges were highly exaggerated, he was sick of listening to her perpetual nagging complaints and of reproaches of his business friends and well-wishers. He decided finally that keeping in mind his own prestige, he would better sell the old house and buy a new one in a new locality.

One day Naushad broached the subject to his father, "Abboo, this house is in a locality of low-level people. It is also far from decent. Hence I have a plan to buy a new flat in a newly-developed colony for which I'll have to sell it. With the proceeds of this old house, with some money from my own savings plus a little loan from the bank, I can buy a new flat and all of us together could stay well in it."

Safdar Khan thought over it a great deal, looked around the house, the ceiling and then gradually began, "I had built up this house with my sweat and blood and no less with those of your mother who is no more now. I took its care as delicately as I had taken care of you. My soul is in it. Now you want to sell it and, I feel, it will be like selling a part of me." After a few minutes with tears in his eyes, he added, "My favourite emperor Shahjahan had constructed a mausoleum like Taj Mahal in the memory of his wife Mumtaj. Now you wish to destroy even a token of the memory of my dead wife Aamna – which is what this house has been. But I am quite old and alone. The house has already been transferred to your name. Since you have the whole life to live whereas I had had my innings, you may do what you feel best for both of you and your children."

The atmosphere became as heavy as a rain-soaked blanket. Allowing a few moments for his father to be normal, Naushad said, "Father, my wife and I cannot live in this house and we cannot leave you alone here. Hence I hope you would not mind if we shift you to the Old Age Home for a week or so. I already had a talk with the Manager."

When Safdar Khan met the inmates of the Old Age Home, his despondency diminished a little in seeing so many people of his own age, particularly as they greeted him by calling him a new member of the Home. He said to others with a sense of pride, "I am here for only one week. My son is buying a new flat in a new colony. Afterwards, he would take me there."

There were mysterious smiles over their faces but Safdar Khan could not understand why should they behave like that. He had full faith in his son. However, some cracks began to appear in his confidence when his son demanded one more weeks' time, and then yet another week's time, for settling down in the new house. Afterwards, Naushad told his father of his impending visit abroad and then his mobile number was no longer working. Safdar Khan still had faith in his son though other inmates of the Home indirectly told him that that his son had gone away from him for good.

Many months passed. In the first week, Safdar Khan missed his house 'Samna' day and night since it was named out of their joint names – Safdar and Aamna – remembered his life with his wife, his love for his son and grandchildren, laced with his daughter-in-law's caustic remarks but gradually he realised that he has to spend his remaining life in the Old Age Home and must reconcile himself to it.

Once Kirti Prakash came to Safdar Khan in the Old Age Home. Safdar happily told him about Naushad's visit to some foreign country but Kirti kept quiet. When Safdar Khan questioned him further about his knowledge of it, Kirti said, "Chacha Jaan, he is all well here in a new flat. I saw him only yesterday."

No words were spoken. Some words are better not spoken. There were telltale signs of disappointment over Safdar Khan's face. He could not understand why his real son had deceived him. Was he such a burden on his son's family despite his monthly pension? Almost spontaneously, his tears peeped through his eyes. Still having a sense of disbelief in what Kirti had said, Safdar Khan asked, "Kirti, my son, I hope you are not teasing me? You used to tease me so much in the past. Tell me the truth. It is difficult to believe that my own son, blood of my own blood, could cheat me."

Comforting Safdar Khan by affectionately patting his drooping shoulders, Kirti Prakash said, "I did not want to reveal this fact to you, Chacha Jaan, but pleasant uncertainty is worse than unpleasant certainty. It is better to swallow a bitter pill once than to be afraid of it all the time. Please don't feel bad about it. You ask these inmates by placing a hand over their hearts, and half of them will tell you tales identical to yours. It is true I am your distant, but visible son, like the moon, but I will always visit you periodically. You and Aamna aunty in the past have been of great help to us, much more than our closest relations have been. I cannot forget those difficult times. Today I have come to invite you, as our family always did in the past, for the Shradha dinner of your friend and my father every year.

Tomorrow is his Shradha. Good things will be prepared and I thought since you might not receive these things in the Old Age Home, I'll come tomorrow, take you to my place for meals and afterwards, leave you here. My father's soul will be happy."

The next day as Kirti Prakash reached the Old Age Home to take him, Safdar Khan begged, "Do me one more favour Kirti. Please take me first for a minute to my old house 'Samna.' I want to see and touch it. My wife's soul will be happy."

Wiping off the old man's leaking eyes, Kirti Prakash took him to his old house. Safdar Khan touched it nostalgically many times and then applied its invisible dust to his forehead. When they reached his home and were seated, Kirti Prakash asked, "Chacha Jaan, probably you love your house as much as your favorite emperor Shahjahan did the Taj Mahal. Can I call it your wife's Taj Mahal?"

"More than that Kirti because it was made by both of us."

"Chacha Jaan," Kirti Prakash continued somewhat humorously. "Mumtaz is believed to have released one of the two prized fantail pigeons of Shahjahan which made him fall in love with her. Do you remember any such story about your pre-marriage life?"

There were obvious signs of glow over Safdar Khan's face as if the past were revisiting him. Closing his eyes for a moment, he began, "Before our marriage, I went to see Aamna. Since she had passed 2nd standard with Hindi medium, I took a simple test by asking her to write Hindi alphabet and she wrote it well. It was all correct but... " Safdar Khan had an uncontrollable laughter.

"What was so funny about it?"

"None could read it," Safdar Khan clarified. "It was written from right to left as one writes Urdu. Later on, her father explained that each time she begins to write one has to tell her whether to write from left or right and that makes all the difference; except for that, she has a photographic memory. When she writes from right to left, you can read it only through a mirror."

Safdar Khan came back to the Old Age Home very happy and satisfied after the sumptuous dinner. The occasion of his friend's Shradha was also an occasion for exchanging news and gossips of old neighbours, friends and relations. He had been in the Old Age Home for nearly nine months' time and it was for the first time he had had such a delicious meal. His Eid and Moharram had gone totally unnoticed. It was late in the night when a cheerful Safdar Khan entered his room humming a tune and fell asleep immediately. In the middle of the night, the rich food made him thirsty; he got up and drank the little water that the clayey pitcher had. At three in the night, he felt still more thirsty but the pitcher was empty. He hesitated in calling any other inmate of the Home for water. His thirst and sleeplessness triggered old memories and he remembered that his favourite emperor Shahjahan had suffered worse fate than he was having. Despite being an emperor, he was imprisoned in a cell for seven long years by his own son Aurangzeb. Over and above, he was given very little water in a somewhat leaky claycy pitcher. Tears came to Safdar Khan's eyes when he recalled a Persian quatrain of Shahjahan which he had sent to his son Aurangzeb:

"Yay pisar too azab Musalmani,
Ba pidaray zindaa aab tarsaani,
Aafreen baad Hindwan sad baar,
Main dehdam pidaray murdarawa daayam aab."

It could be rendered into English as:

"My son, you are a strange Muslim who is making your living father tantalizingly thirsty for water. Praise be the Hindus thousands of times who offer water to their ancestors even many years after their death."

❖❖❖

11

EXPIATION

Dheeraj Lal was a grocery shop owner who had two daughters. His wife Indravati took care of the family and at the same time also managed the agricultural land, inherited from her father, now given to tenant farmers. Bhoori Bai was a maidservant who swept the house and cleaned the grocery items for Dheeraj Lal's shop and as such was given a room in the sprawling house in which she lived with her son Umang.

As a good-will gesture, Dheeraj Lal got Umang admitted to a Hindi medium school in the neibhbourhood. Indravati, his wife, vehemently opposed his act of spending even a small amount of money on his education, "Why educate the boy?" She burst out. "It will add some more airs to the family."

Dheeraj Lal's elder daughter Annapurna was nine years old and studied in the 4th standard while her younger sister Vijaya was in the second. Both went to an English medium school in an auto rickshaw. Annapurna always concealed some cookies, sweets or chocolates in her school bag. As a result of Annapurna's habit of over-eating, she started putting on weight while Vijaya remained slim and attractive. When it came to classroom performance, Annapurna often slept in the class while Vijaya remained among the top five position-holders. Later on, Annapurna failed in the examination.

When Anna was scolded on her failure by her mother, she laughed and said almost in a shameless manner, "I have saved your money, Amma. You wouldn't have to buy new books for me."

Umang was roughly of the same age as Vijaya but he was studying in one class junior to her. To satisfy his curiosity, Umang asked her many questions which puzzled her. He would look blankly into the sky without looking at anything in particular and ask many puzzling questions, such as, why do the sky and the earth seem to meet at the horizon? Why do river and ocean appear filled with blue water? How did the inventor of the first clock set the correct time on his clock? Vijaya often wondered how much curiosity and thinking capacity Umang had! While Vijaya helped Umang in the text books of Hindi and English languages, he was so good in mathematics that he even helped Vijaya in solving some difficult sums. Many times Vijaya thought if Umang only had reasonably well-to-do parents, he could have obtained good education.

While Annapurna remained preoccupied with nibbling something or other, Umang and Vijaya often played different games together. Indravati asked her not to associate or play with him since he was the son of their maidservant and belonged to a lower vegetable-growing caste, but Vijaya paid no attention to it.

It was some festival on which Indravati asked both Umang and his mother Bhoori Bai for meals. Vijaya had the habit of asking some simple yet tricky questions from Umang just to tease him. Since he also knew that he was being teased, he too did not answer them straightway. She asked him, "Umang, suppose you had nine hundred ninety nine rupees and you spent one hundred fourteen out of them, how much money would be left with you?"

Umang laughed an idiotic laugh and said, "First of all, I would not have so much money and, secondly, I would not spend any money without my mother's permission."

Since Umang was taking meals, Indravati cautioned, "Vijaya, let him take his food. Don't trouble him."

Ignoring her mother's warning, Vijaya asked another question, "Suppose you had two chapattis and you ate both of them. What will be left?"

"Rice and vegetable curry."

Indravati shouted, "Vijaya, you are hitting your head against the wall; these low-caste people cannot learn anything even though the government is giving them all facilities. They are not made for this purpose."

Being in charge of agricultural land and tenant farmers, Indravati invited for dinner either the Superintendent of Police or District Collector once or twice a year so that she could impress neighbours and bully the tenant farmers. One day after the new District Collector was invited, Indravati came to know that he belonged to the untouchable caste of leather workers. Conscious of being a Brahmin, she wanted to cancel the invitation but Vijaya advised her that the cancellation would amount to an insult of the Collector who could revengefully harm the family

Realising that she would have to honour the invitation, Indravati felt that the best course for her would be not to use her own utensils but to borrow those of Umang's family but Vijaya objected to it again on the plea that their utensils could be far from being decent for such an officer. Such people are extremely sensitive to insults in various ways and it might be counterproductive. Indravati agreed to it but insisted that in case she used her own utensils, Vijaya would have to clean them.

After the District Collector had left, Vijaya was asked to clean the used utensils by placing them first in the midst of dung-fire, and after allowing them to cool down, they were given to Bhoori Bai to scrub and slosh them since she belonged to the vegetable-seller's caste and hence was touchable even if she too was below her own Brahmin caste. Afterwards, the utensils were washed by Vijaya before allowing their entry back into the kitchen.

Giggling loudly, Vijaya asked, "Amma, if the utensils need a fire-purification, what about chairs and tables used by him? Are you not going to give them a similar fire-test? Our great Sita was also given a fire test."

"Shut up, Vijaya," Indravati scolded affectionately. "Do as you have been told."

One day Vijaya and Umang were playing with a rubber ball by chasing and hitting each other with it. Indravati was cutting vegetables with a large knife. Vijaya threw the ball at Umang but it hit the wall, bounced and hit her mother. Stopping her work, Indravati shouted at Vijaya, "It would have cut my hand, you fool!" Feeling angry, she threw the knife at Vijaya which would have hit her nose but Umang caught it just in time. In the process, his finger was deeply cut. He was immediately taken to the Government hospital where a surgeon stitched it. It took a little over one month for the finger to be healed but it remained somewhat bent. Vijaya expressed her gratitude to Umang for saving her nose from being disfigured.

Whenever Vijaya went to see Umang's finger and helped him in dressing it up, Indravati became angry and asked her,

"Why do you associate so much with the low-caste lad? It is not desirable for the people of Brahmin caste!"

"And it is alright for the Brahmins to cut their daughter's nose and the finger of a low-caste lad."

"Shut up, you impertinent girl!" Indravati became angry. "Why don't you begin to live in that room of his?"

"I will if need be," Vijaya spoke in the same tone.

For a couple of days, so much of tension pervaded in the house that one could almost touch it. Indravati thought that Umang was responsible for it. Keeping in mind how Vijaya had begun to take Umang's side against her very mother, she went on looking for an opportunity to throw him out of the servant's room because she thought he was an evil in embryo.

The opportunity came sooner than expected. After the incident of the rubber ball, Umang and Vijaya were warned never to play with the rubber ball. Abandoning the rubber ball, Umang made a ball of discarded rags which were tied around and reinforced by tightly criss crossing pieces of rope around it so that it retained its rounded shape. As against the rubber ball which bounced on hitting any hard surface, the rag-ball did not – or bounced almost negligibly.

Complacently and without fear of hitting anybody, Vijaya and Umang played with the rag-ball in the open yard outside the house. Umang threw the ball very fast in order to hit Vijaya. As she dodged the ball, it went straight through the passage to the inner yard, hit the wall and plumped into the vegetable curry in the bronze plate of Indravati as she was eating.

Indravati saw the ball, which was made obviously of unhygienic and dirty rags and which must already have fallen at several unclean places. To have such a ball in her vegetable curry was like the landing of a hand grenade after the removal of the pin and one could only wait with suspended breath for the explosion to take place any moment.

While both Vijaya and Umang remained cowering before Indravati's cool temperament, they knew that it was the deceptive lull before the storm. She washed her hands, folded them before the plate as if apologising to the Goddess of food for abandoning the blessed meal midway because it had become dirty. Then she went straight to the servant's room in which Umang and his mother were staying and without exchanging a word, began to throw various items of the room outside, shouting to Umang, "Tell your mother to find a room elsewhere."

Vijaya begged her mother not to do so while Umang began to cry. His mother came and lay down prostrate on the ground, touching Indravati's feet and begging forgiveness but the latter refused to yield. A servant was called to throw all items outside the bounds of the house. When Dheeraj Lal was called, he too attempted to persuade his wife to realise how important Bhoori Bai was for the reputation of the grocery shop but Indravati remained adamant on her decision.

Crying convulsively, Vijaya begged the mother repeatedly not to expel Umang, but Indravati said, "My decision is final. They must leave the room."

❖❖❖

Many years passed. During this period, Annapurna had become quite bulky. Many marriageable young men, invited to see her, had refused to select her for a wife. They ran away from her presence as if she had some visible infectious disease. Nevertheless, Annapurna remained blissfully unmindful of such things and continued munching edible things most of the time.

Some problems had arisen with the delimitation of agricultural land. Indravati waited anxiously for the next District Collector to come as the problem was beyond the powers of the Deputy Collector. As soon as the new District Collector joined the post, Vijaya was sent to invite him for the dinner.

When Vijaya went to the office of the District Collector, the name plate of Umang Kushwaha rang some bells within her. Could he be the same person who was living in the servant's room of her house! No. That was impossible. She had absolutely no idea where her childhood playmate might be or what he might be doing. If Umang had a good family and education, like hers, he possibly could have become the District Collector from OBC quota and the name could really have belonged to him. But there was no use in thinking of such things. Her line of thought was broken when she was called inside. For a moment, Vijaya could not believe her eyes. It was the same Umang, one-time playmate of her childhood.

"How are you Vijaya?" Umang welcomed her warmly. It was undoubtedly the same face, the same voice; there was no mistaking it. "I was planning to visit your house but you have called me even earlier. How is Amma? And Annapurna? She must have got married by now?"

"Everyone is fine. I am so relieved to see you in this position. All these years there has been a feeling of guilt over me that I could do nothing when your household items were being thrown out."

"That is all over," Umang said smilingly. "Sometimes things happen for the best. I would not have been what I am today but for Amma's anger. After a couple of days of wanderings, my mother got a job of a maidservant in the house of a rich man who had no issues. He considered me his son, gave me education and now you see me here."

When Vijaya informed her mother about Umang, it was absolutely unbelievable for her, almost like a fairy tale of rags to riches. As Umang visited them for dinner, he touched Amma's feet. With a feeling of guilt, Indravati said, "My son, you know when I become angry, I don't look around. After a couple of days, we searched but you were nowhere to be found."

After the dinner when Umang began to carry his utensils himself for washing, saying, "I would wash them as I did in the past."

Indravati snatched them from his hands and laughingly said, "You are the king of the district now, my boy. How can I commit this sin of letting you wash your utensils? We are sorry for what we made you do in your childhood."

"Amma," Umang said, touching her feet again while going back to his residence. "I am thankful for whatever you did for us in the past and I would be happy to do whatever I can for you."

When a proposal was sent through Vijaya to Umang to get married to Annapurna, he gently declined with the excuse that he had always considered her his elder sister and hence he could not marry her, but he was willing to get married to Vijaya. This infuriated Indravati and she blew up, "How could that low-caste man dare to ask for a Brahmin girl's hand!"

"Do you mean to say that Annapurna, whom you wanted him to marry, is not a Brahmin girl?" Vijay asked but her mother remained quiet.

Laden with the guilt of her mother's ill-treatment of Umang in the past, obliged to him for saving her nose from being sliced with her mother's knife even at the cost of his own finger, Vijaya continued to visit Umang stealthily and remained in touch with him over her mobile. After Umang was transferred to a remote distsrict of the State, Vijaya disappeared from her house, got married to him in the court, and informed her mother subsequently. It was, she thought, an expiation for the sins of the family.

❖❖❖

12

A GREAT PRIZE

Being a free-lance writer, not attached to any paper in particular, Chinmaya Prajapati wrote articles, middles, interviews and short sketches for various newspapers, journals and magazines; in return, he received payments for them. The basic difficulty in the profession was that he had no regular income; it was either feast or fast. The payments that he received were rather small in proportion to the labour he was putting in his job but what sustained him was that his name was being respectfully taken as a rising star in the world of newspaper correspondents. Occasionally, there were prizes too for various items.

When Chinmaya Prajapati brought a wad of new, crisp fifty-rupee currency notes from the bank after encashing one such prize cheque of five thousand rupees, he was very happy because the prize was received for highlighting the cases of social injustice and was given by the Watchdog of Social Justice – a non-government organisation. Besides, the new currency notes had always held a great fascination for him and when it was a wad of 100 such new notes, his pleasure and excitement knew no bounds. He felt he would not like to spend any one of them.

However, much against his wishes, he had already planned to pay his overdue house rent as well as electricity and milkman's bills out of the prize money. A small part of the amount was to go to his wife Rohini who firmly believed that if the prize was awarded to Chinmaya, it was due to her devotion to god for which she must perform certain religious rituals. But before using the new currency notes, he would like to show a trick with them to his son Sukumar.

Thinking on how to budget the prize money, Chinmaya sat down in a corner seat of a *dhaba,* sipping a cup of tea. He quietly brought out the wad of new currency notes and played with it. Pressing half of it with his left palm, he raised the other end with his thumb and released them one by one with lightning speed with a k-r-r-r-r sound as the playing cards make when they are shuffled and reshuffled. In doing so, he found that Gandhi's picture and other details on them remained steady and unchanged but the last digit of the number changed so rapidly that it appeared to dance. This is what he was going to show to his son Sukumar and then explain how multiple still pictures with minor changes become moving in cinemas. As he was doing so, he noticed that at a little short distance away from him something was attracting many onlookers. Putting the wad back into his bag and finishing his tea hurriedly, he reached the place of crowd and noticed that a lady in tattered sari and blouse sat near the flowing gutter with her two children. Taking dirty water from it, she was feeding to her children – first to her son and then to her daughter. While some of the people began to discuss about it, a few others made videos with their mobiles.

Seeing her miserable condition, Chinmaya Prajapati felt pity over her and asked, "Why are you giving dirty gutter water to your children?"

She told him she had pathetically begged for food and water everywhere, particularly from hotel and restaurant owners, but each one of them had shooed her away. She herself could bear hunger and thirst, but not that of her small children. Hence she had fed the gutter water to them.

Taking one crisp fifty-rupee note from the prize money, he immediately purchased a bottle of mineral water and gave it to her. Gogi let the children drink water liberally from it and then emptied the remaining part of the bottle herself. Feeling deeply concerned, Chinmaya took them to a *dhaba* and requested them to eat anything while he would pay for their meals.

As Gogi and her children were taking food, she told Chinmaya her pathetic, heart-rending tale. She was from a village on the outskirts of Kohima in Nagaland. Her husband had died after struggling with illness for seven months. As a daily labour, she was earning barely forty rupees per day, the major part of which was spent on his treatment. After seven months of illness, he passed away. It was a great shock to her. She did not have even a penny with her for his last rites, and consequently, his dead body lay in the hut.

It remained lying in the hut for many hours while Gogi went from house to house and person to person, seeking some money on loan so that the last rites of her husband could be performed but since everyone knew her miserable condition, none was willing to lend her any amount.

Finally, she went to Inamdar – a money-lender of the area who was notoriously known to be cunning and merciless in his dealings. He too knew her miserable condition and her problems in returning the loaned amount. However, being an expert in his money-lending business, he said, "Gogi, my daughter, you know that you cannot pay back the money easily. Since the body of your husband is lying in the hut, I feel rather bad about it. Nothing can be worse than that. Hence I can loan you two thousand rupees which you want but for that you will have to agree to my condition."

Trembling over his possible demand, she nervously asked, "What is the condition?"

With a crooked smile over his face, he explained, "You will have to pledge your eight-year old son as security. He will do the work for me as long as you do not pay back the money. The moment you do so, you can take your son back. Since the amount is for the last rites of your husband, I'll not be so mean as to charge any interest on it."

Gogi thought for quite sometime. She had no land, no gold or silver ornaments, no metallic utensils, and no brick-house which she could have pledged in lieu of her son. She had a grass-covered hut with wooden and baked mud-utensils or, at most, a few aluminum pots and pans. During the illness of her husband, her eight-year-old son was the only source of help to her. He also used to take care of her five-year old daughter and three-year old son. Being the eldest son, he was the apple of her eye on whom all the future hopes of the entire family rested, particularly now that her husband was no more. She did not want to keep him as a mortgage and suggested an alternative by praying earnestly, "By agreeing to loan me two thousand rupees, you have come out as a god to me. Kindly be a little more kind, sir, by taking any one of my remaining two children in place of my eldest son. He is my right hand. After my husband's death, being the eldest male member in the family, he has been shouldering all responsibilities of the family and I cannot do anything without him."

Shaking his head in the negative, Inamdar said to her, "What good are the other two children to me? Your eldest boy will at least do small things for me."

Realising that her husband's dead body was lying in the hut, she thought she had no choice. The urgency demanded that the last rites of the dead body of her husband be performed as long as there was daylight. Wiping her tears, she took the money from him and promised to send her son to him after the last rites.

After all the rituals were performed and every penny of the borrowed money spent, Gogi's big worry was how to pay back two thousand rupees and to get her son released? Her daily wage of forty rupees was hardly enough for the survival of her family. The eldest son used to earn some money as a helper, but he too was gone.

She knew she did not have much chance of saving two thousand rupees in Nagaland – certainly not in the near future. Since her other relations were leaving Nagaland for U.P. for better wages, she along with her two children landed in Agra. For the whole day, all of them wandered from place to place and shop to shop but got no work. With the promise of coming back soon, her relations quietly disappeared, leaving her and her two small children alone. Since Chinmaya had saved her and her children from hunger and thirst, she blessed him profusely in her own dialect with a couple of Hindi words, part of which he understood.

So far Chinmaya had spent a couple of new fifty-rupee currency notes on them. Rather than doing anything further, Chinmaya thought it desirable to take them to the Superintendent of Police so that the latter could contact his counterpart in Kohima to ensure that she was telling the truth and that the money-lender would restore her son after receiving the payment of two thousand rupees. He was also hopeful that the Superintendent of Police would make arrangement for her travel to Kohima along with some money for the release of her son but the police officer merely contacted his counterpart in Kohima and ensured that Gogi's son would be restored after she makes the requisite payment.

The Superintendent of Police thanked Chinmaya for taking care of the destitute family and requested him further to see that the family was well-seated in the train. Gogi's clothes were quite torn with several holes in her multi-patched saree and blouse out of which her breasts peeped frequently and so were the clothes of her children. Feeling pity over them, Chinmaya purchased some clothes for them.

Taking them to the railway station, Chinmaya bought a train ticket for Gogi. No tickets were needed for the children. Now over half of the wad of new currency notes was spent. He could still show the trick with them to his son but he remembered he had to pay Gogi two thousand rupees for the release of her son. With a heavy heart, he counted forty of them amounting to two thousand rupees and gave them to Gogi for her son's release from the money-lender.

Out of the entire wad, only one last fifty-rupee note was left with him. He nostalgically held the lone, crisp, unfolded currency note with his fingers, wondering what would his wife and son say to him? What would happen to the payment of his outstanding house rent and other bills? Then he looked at Gogi and her children, wondering what would they eat and drink in their long journey to Kohima? Realising that the fifty-rupee note alone could serve him no purpose, he handed it to Gogi who was already greedily gazing at it.

As the train began to move, he saw Gogi folding her son's. daughter's and her own hands to say good bye to Chinmaya with tears peeping from her eyes. He too became emotional and waved his hand back in response while walking a few steps by the side of the moving compartment. As the train became out of sight, he walked back towards his home.

Recollecting the incidents of the entire day, particularly of Gogi's problems, he had a bubbling sense of immense ecstasy arising within him as though for saving three – even four – lives of the destitute family, he had got a great prize. The pleasure was so much that it filled his heart with inexplicable emotions of satisfaction as if his heart were a gas-filled balloon or as if he were walking in the air with light, springy feet, much above the common pedestrians below, forgetting the payment of overdue rent and pending bills, oblivious of the amount he had promised to pay to his wife, and not even recollecting the trick he wanted to show to his son.

❖❖❖

13

CORRIDOR THERAPY

At the age of fifty, Lalita felt happy that a grandson was born to her and that he was as fair and beautiful as she herself was in her young age. It was a living incarnation of her concept of beauty. She was very proud of her grandson Rohit and breathlessly told her friends and relations that her beauty was duplicated into him.

Since her son and daughter-in-law were in jobs in a private company and were inexperienced in bringing up the child, Lalita took care of the newly-born son after a couple of weeks. Though she and her husband Ved Ram lived in the village Lakhanpur of Meerut district, they lovingly took care of Rohit. Lalita massaged him well, gave him bath, dressed him well and took complete care of him. Her son and his wife visited the village occasionally on Sundays and were very happy to see that Rohit had a good time with his grandparents and hence continued to do their jobs without any problem.

As the child Rohit grew a little, he was sent back to his parents in Meerut because now he could be handled by them. Lalita's initial care was like that of the early care of a seedling which usually has a high mortality rate. As a grandmother, Lalita wanted to accompany Rohit to Meerut but the house in which her son Om Pal was living was rather small. Within his small salary, he could not afford a large house but Lalita drew a promise that whenever they found any problem, Rohit would be sent to the village again.

When Rohit reached the age of four, he was sent once more to his grandparents in the village because his mother fell ill and was hospitalised. For Lalita and her husband Ved Ram, Rohit was a welcome member, no less than a VIP who brought happiness in their lives. Considering him a living toy, they fondled him, talked to him, imitating his halting, prattling way of talking which made even the neighbours happy.

In the village, Rohit enjoyed what to the urban people appear exotic items. He rode on the cow or buffalo, ran and jumped with the newly born calves, enjoyed watching the milking of cows and buffaloes, sat on the shoulders of the cowherd, plucked various kinds of fruits and flowers, washed his hands and feet in the thick stream of the tube well and looked with wonder on the green crops of wheat and rice.

In the mornings, both Lalita and Ved Ram used to have a cup of tea. Rohit too wished to have one. When a half-filled cup of tea was given to him, he placed it on the floor, rushed in excitement to his grandmother, shouting, "Dadiji. Dadiji,, the cup has fever. Bring that thermometer with which you had measured Dadu's fever."

Lalita picked him in her arms, kissed him repeatedly and said, "Cups don't have fever, my little son; only men, women and children have."

"What about cows and buffaloes?" Rohit asked innocently. "Do they have fever?"

This was a puzzling question to the grandmother and she gave an indirect reply, "Even if they have, we have never come across the fevering animals."

After preparing and serving meals in the night, Lalita or Ved Ram would often narrate a number of tales from *Panchatantra,* the *Ramayana* or the *Mahabharata* which Rohit enjoyed. When the condition of his mother in the city became better, Rohit reluctantly went back to Meerut where he was admitted to school. It was from that time onwards that his visits to the village were drastically cut short because the schooling became more important than anything else.

❖❖❖

Lalita was now eighty years old. A series of illnesses had made her quite weak. Her grandson Rohit was now a married young man who had a good job with a high salary and kept her in a beautiful, well-furnished room. Lalita's husband Ved Ram, her only son Om Pal and his wife had died in a car accident and now she as the sole survivor stayed with her grandson.

Rohit had vivid memories of his childhood spent in the village with his grandparents, as also of the love that his grandmother Lalita used to bestow on him. He remembered too how he was fond of toy cars and how his grandmother used to bare her tummy which due to acidity used to swell like a smooth, shining balloon on which Rohit, as a child, would place cars one by one and then would allow them to roll down. The disease of Lalita was such that after an hour or so of her taking midday or evening meal, her tummy would swell painlessly like a balloon, a little less in size than that of a football. Then gradually, she would press and squeeze her hands and feet and as a result of which the burping and belching sounds would emanate from her mouth which would gradually un-swell the tummy till it came to its normal size.

Now after thirty years, Lalita was quite aged and ill, and things had changed a great deal. Remembering vividly every moment of his childhood spent in the village, Rohit wished to compensate his grandmother, particularly in the absence of his own parents and his grandfather. He selected the quietest room on the first floor, got it fitted with an Air Conditioner, purchased the most expensive curtains for the door and the window, and had two or three call bells fitted at various places, including the toilet, so that in the hour of need, she could press it from any place without any need of shouting and he, his wife, his children or the maid would rush there to help her. A colour television with a large screen was fitted to the wall of her room which she could operate with a remote control. He also got the best physician in Meerut who visited her once or twice a week. Unfortunately, her condition continued to deteriorate slowly as though the treatment had no effect on her. Later, her body refused to respond to the best treatment available and she became so weak that she could hardly get up from her bed.

When such a thing went on for a couple of months, the physician apologised, "I am sorry, Rohit ji, I have done all I could, but she is not responding to the treatment. To me the disease seems to be from within. It appears as if she has abandoned the desire to live and no medicines work under such circumstances."

Lalita remained alone in the room, thinking of the past which was now no more. Rohit came two times a day to her – before going and after coming back from work and so did his wife. Their children – one boy of six years and a daughter of four years did drop in occasionally to pick up their rubber ball which happened to drift to the terrace in front of her room. Lalita felt happy in seeing both the great grandchildren though occasionally she heard their voices when they played either in the house or outside. She yearned to see them, to hold them, to touch them as she used to do her grandson Rohit in his childhood, but she was now too weak to get up and counted her days for the last journey. She thanked god that while her other senses were failing, her sense of hearing was somewhat better. In the games of children, in their shouts and yells, she nostalgically revisited the past when her grandson Rohit was a child and used to play the same way, particularly with his toy cars on her swollen stomach.

Disturbed somewhat while sitting with his grandmother, Rohit was nearly heart-broken and wailed, "Dadiji, I don't know what to do. I know you must be remembering the tragic deaths of Dadaji, and my parents and you know I cannot bring them back. I too feel bad about them. All I have now is you, and for you I am doing all I can but the medicines of the best doctors have no effect on you."

Lalita touched his forehead and softly consoled, "Rohit, don't worry about me. My time has come. I have no repentance. I have lived a good life. Where else could I have found so much of happiness after the passing away of your Dada ji, your own father and mother? I am so happy and satisfied with what you have done and are doing for me. Since the medicines have no effect on my ailment, it simply implies that my last days are here and I would like to live the way I like."

"Is there anything that I or my wife has not done for you?"

"No. Rohit, you and your wife have done everything," Lalita asserted. "Look at this room. Is it in any way less than that of a queen? What is there which this room lacks? Now that the medicines are having no effect on me, would you be good enough to fulfil my one last wish?"

Holding her bony hands, Rohit said pathetically with tears in his eyes, "Dadi ji, just tell me and I would do anything you say."

"Then shift my bed to the corridor on the ground floor."

"To the corridor?" Rohit felt shocked. "There can be no facilities – no Air-conditioner, no television, no privacy, no peace. No second cot can be placed there for the nurse in case of need. You may have no rest or sleep because all kinds of noises reach there. Our children and those of neighbours play so boisterously that you would not have even a good hour's sleep in day time. I cannot give there any of the comforts that you find in this room."

Lalita smiled and said, "There is the whole night for me to take rest and to sleep. Remember Rohit, I come from the village where I lived the simplest sort of life without electricity. Hence let me live now as I wish."

Rohit appealed, "Dadi ji, please think again. It is not a very good place for you. But since you wish it, I cannot say 'no' to you. In such a case, promise me that when you don't feel at home in the corridor, you will come back to this room."

"I assure you my son," Lalita said. "If needed, I will shift to this room, but the occasion would not come. Just wait and see."

As her bed was shifted to the corridor, much against the wishes of her grandson and his wife, Lalita felt very happy. She felt as if she had re-linked herself to the living humanity. In her room on the first floor, the only visible scene was that of the Muslim *kabaristan* (graveyard) in which many caskets of the dead bodies were brought, the graves were dug up and the dead bodies lowered and buried in them. She saw the grief-stricken, drooping heads of their friends and relations. Even when she used to keep her face away from the window, the scene was reflected in the mirror of the steel almirah kept in front of her bed. It was as if there was no escape from the inevitability of death. Each time after the mourners had left, the peace of the graveyard reigned there literally and metaphorically till another dead body arrived. The scene stayed in concrete form in her mind as if she could touch it. When the curtain was drawn on the window to block the view and the light switched off, the dark room appeared as a vast open grave and she as a dead body waiting for the soil to be poured on her. Even the dreams were really nightmares which related to the horrible pictures of deaths and murders in their most gruesome forms. After being shifted to the corridor, she could witness the games that both her great grandchildren played in the inner yard or outside. She saw or heard their giggles, their peals of laughter, their movements, their running around or together and their frequent complaints against each other which they brought to her for arbitration. Life seemed livable now. As the children came, touched and teased her, Lalita enjoyed every moment of their activities.

One day, the boy came running to her in excitement, asking, "Baddi Dadi, I have found a coin. Of how much value is it?"

Lalita scrutinised the coin carefully and found it to be outdated. She said, "*yah chalta naheen*" (it is outdated).

The boy took the coin, played with it with his sister for sometime, and then placed it on Lalita's swollen tummy. Soon it fell down and rolled in a circular motion and the boy said, "Look Dadi ji, *yah chalta hai*" (It moves).

Lalit felt very happy and embraced him. It was as if Rohit as a child had come in the form of her great grandson.

During the whole day when Rohit and his wife were on the job, the activities of the children rejuvenated her drooping spirits. Gradually, she began to get up, to sit on the bed and to enjoy the giggling company of the children. It was as if she were revisiting her own and her grandson's life in the past..

Within one month, Lalita felt recuperating her energy fast. One day, Rohit was surprised to see his grandmother standing up on the ground and throwing the ball at her great grandchildren as it had fallen on her cot.

One month after his sojourn abroad, the physician saw and was unbelievably surprised to see the glow on Lalita's face and the movements of her hands and feet. Fumbling for an explanation, he philosophised, "It is all due to god. What the medicines failed to do, god's blessings did it. Or did you change to some other treatment – I mean, Ayurvedic or Homeopathic therapy?"

"Doctor Sahib," Lalita broke in before Rohit could say anything to the physician. "It is because of the shifting of my bed to the corridor where I interact with all the living people, particularly children, physically and ocularly, while I was all alone in the room above looking at the Muslim graveyard. I would say that it is neither Homeopathic, Ayurvedic nor Allopathic but what has brought a transformation in my health and spirits is the corridor therapy.

❖❖❖

14

SOWING SEEDS

Shuchita was a school teacher who lived with her husband Alankrit Manharan in Gorakhpur. She taught in a private school but her real interest remained in gardening both in the school and at home. Her husband was an Office Assistant in a private company. Both of them earned enough money to carry on their livelihood with dignity. What made them happy was their goodness of temperament and their interest in gardening.

They had a small house which Shuchita Manharan decorated with her own hands and felt a strange pleasure in doing so. Since she did not have any child of her own, she was fond of others' children and helped them in school and outside. If a need arose, she did not hesitate in buying books and in paying their fees, particularly if they happened to be poor.

Many times Alankrit counseled, "Shuchita, your habit of liberally helping the boys and girls is an undoubtedly laudable exercise, but please do remember that the world is quite selfish and none might come forward to help you or me in our hour of need."

"I agree, Alankrit, with you, but it gives me a great pleasure. Besides, someone had told me once that if you throw a handful of seeds anywhere and if all of them happen to die but just one germinates and grows into a tree, it would pay many times its labour and cost."

In the mornings and evenings, Shuchita took care of the plants whose blooming flowers attracted the attention of a large number of passersby. She liberally gave away flowers to them while their full-throated praise filled her heart with inexplicable pleasure as if they were praising her children.

Shuchita also had a beautiful lawn which was well-mown by her and her husband. Surrounded by plants with multi-coloured flowers, it looked so beautiful that once a monthly magazine titled *House Garden* took her permission to use its colour photo on their cover page. Afterwards, the visits of others to her house began to multiply and people asked her several questions about the availability of flower plants, their seeds, the method of sowing and maintaining them, and the use of manure and fertilizer. With the publication of the picture on the cover of the magazine, overnight Shuchita became a very important person in the locality. However, the wide publicity and comments of the visitors failed to add an iota of pride in her nature. Whenever anyone sought guidance, she gave numerous tips for the maintenance of the front lawn and the flower plants.

Though her husband did praise her for her perspicuity but at the same time, he periodically cautioned her that the people are selfish and that she might have to repent later for her open-heartedness. The best thing was to save some money for the rainy day.

"My deeds are my riches," Shuchita Manharan clarified. "As I help others, I feel a genuine sense of that inexplicable ecstasy which the act of saving money does not. Besides, it is a very small amount of salary which I spend on the needy children."

After a couple of years, they realized that Alankrit was suddenly losing his weight very rapidly. They consulted a physician who got his detailed investigations done. It was found that he had the dreaded disease of leukemia – blood cancer.

It was a great shock for both of them, particularly for Shuchita. He was all she had; there were no children and none who could advance them money on loan for his treatment. Whatever money was there in the bank was exhausted very fast in a series of investigations and in visiting various hospitals. They had no relations rich and generous enough who could advance them some money.

When a large amount of money was needed, going into a couple of lakhs for Alankrit's treatment, with a heavy heart, they had to mortgage their house for three lakh rupees with a rider that in case they failed to return the amount by a stipulated date, the house will be treated as sold. Meanwhile, they could continue to stay on in the house on payment of a fixed monthly rent.

It was the second shock of Shuchita's life. After knowing of her husband's disease, the house which she had nourished with the same love and care as one gives one's own child was now slipping away from her hands. The only fading hope was that someday, when the husband gets cured of his illness, both of them would work very hard and earn money enough to reclaim the house. Unfortunately, she had to spend all the money from the proceeds of the mortgage while her husband, instead of getting cured, succumbed to the disease.

The husband's death was the greatest shock of Shuchita's life and she was totally shaken to her roots. It certainly brought to her a large number of sympathizers who inundated her with their supportive and encouraging words, making her feel considerably consoled by bringing down the intensity of the sorrow of bereavement but she found nothing substantial in their words which might have raised her hope of freeing the house from mortgage.

There were many persons among them whose children she had helped financially and thought that they would come forward to reciprocate her past magnanimity; but such a thing did not take place. She certainly felt good that her kind acts were being remembered but there also arose a black shadow of pain that had she saved all the money she had given away by way of helping others, particularly to children, probably she would not have been required to mortgage the house. The difficulty was that she had also retired from school service because of superannuation.

There were times when Shuchita wondered why was god punishing her so much when she had done nothing but good for others? The impression she gathered from others was that one is rewarded or punished for his or her good and bad activities in this life itself. Then why was god not doing anything to help her in this life?

The locality was buzzing with rumours that a new person had re-purchased some of the houses including her own and that he was very strict and unrelenting in the realisation of dues. He did not condone even one day's delay in payment of rent. In a case or two, due to the delay of a couple of days, eviction notices were served and finally within fifteen days, their household items were thrown on the street. Hence the agent had warned the tenants again and again either to pay the rent on time, vacate the house or to face eviction.

The last option was clearly something which was bound to bring shame to the evicted person. Shuchita Manharan had already got the eviction notice and was frantically looking for an alternative accommodation, but they were all very expensive and she did not have much money. Being an old teacher, she used to do the private coaching of students but that was merely good enough to make both ends meet. The only option left for her was to go to the Old Age Home in Gorakhpur in which there was no vacancy immediately but it was likely to be there within a couple of days.

Fifteen days after the eviction notice was served, the agent came and began to put Shuchita's belongings on the road. When she begged him to give her two or three days more during which she would sell her household items and move to the Old Age Home, the agent declined to give even one hour. He said the notice period was over and the boss had asked him to throw the belongings on the street.

"Give me just two more days," Shuchita begged.

Without relenting a little, the agent said, "I cannot give you even one minute. Personally, I really would have liked to do so if it were within my powers, but if I do not do so now, Madam, I will be thrown out of my job. I have my wife and children and I would not like to have the same fate as yours."

Though still hopeful that something might come up to help her, she stayed on and began to cry. Some neighbours came and consoled her that they would like to help her but they had no money to spare.

As the agent and his men were keeping her belongings on the road, Shuchita begged again, "Please give me just two days to shift to the Old Age Home."

The agent said, "I am sorry to repeat, Madam, that it is not within my powers to do so. Only the new boss can do so."

She begged again, "Okay. Why don't you convey my request to him?"

"Madam, even I don't know him and besides, I have strict orders that no matter what happens, the house must be vacated by this evening."

The agent and his team began to pick up items of the house and place them on the road. There were tears in the old woman's eyes. Again and again, she prayed to god to save her house from being disrobed, as was Draupadi in the *Mahabharata*. Like the mythological beleaguered lady, Shuchita prayed to god frantically to save her honour and dignity. It was not that she was confident of any help, but the mere act of praying made her feet stand momentarily steady on the ground.

A passerby curiously stopped by her and began to make enquiries about removing the household items. Finding a person more sympathetic than the agent, Shuchita begged him pathetically to persuade the Agent to give her two more days during which she would sell all her household items and start living in the Old Age Home of the city.

The new comer asked the Agent, "Why can't you wait for two days? Don't you know she had helped hundreds of needy children in the past? Now she is in need of help herself and none is ready to do anything for her."

"It is not in my powers, sir," he said. "There are strict orders from the boss to have it vacated by today evening."

"Well," the person said. "What if I order you to place all her household items back into the house?"

"I can't do so, sir. I am sorry."

"You have to," the new comer ordered. "Here are the court papers. She is the owner of the house." Saying this, he gave one copy of the papers to the Agent and the other one to Shuchita.

The Agent saw the court papers and found that there was no ambiguity and that her name "Shuchita Manharan" was clearly written as the owner of the house. He ordered the helpers to place all the household items back into the house.

After the Agent and his men had gone, he asked Shuchita, "Won't you ask me to come inside the house and offer me a cup of tea?"

Completely overwhelmed with tears rolling down her cheeks, Shuchita kneeled down to touch his feet, but he checked and hugged her. Making him comfortably seated in the sofa, she asked, "The entire thing appears as a pleasant dream." Then after a pause, she hesitantly asked, "Are the court papers real?"

"They are genuine, Madam. Have no doubts about them."

"Then how could you do such a great favour to me when I don't even know you?"

"But I know you, Madam," the new comer said. "I am Shyam. Many many years ago, I was studying in a High School. After a long illness my father had died and I, with my mother, a daily labourer, was staying temporarily in half-constructed accommodation at the construction site. I did not have the fees without which I would not have been allowed to appear in the examination. When I begged others for fees, people either ignored my requests, ridiculed me or at most gave me small coins the amount of which was far from adequate. Then some gentleman, overhearing my story, suggested your name. When I narrated my story, you not only gave me adequate funds by simply emptying your purse on the spot but also a tiny brass image of Goddess Lakshmi for good luck. As an expression of gratitude, I had assured you that someday whenever possible I would like to pay you back. The incident took place in front of your husband who did not seem to appreciate your act of helping me but who had remained observing everything without passing a comment. Where is he now?"

It appeared as if the narration had sent her back into the past and after a few seconds, Shuchita said, "Unfortunately, he had had leukemia for the treatment of which I had to mortgage this house. I had decided to go to the Old Age Home in the city. Shyam, you have made me the owner of the house, but I don't have the means to pay its cost."

"You don't have to," Shyam said. "Take it as a gift of a person for whose future you had sowed the seed which has now become a full blown tree. Since you must still be puzzled by what has happened, let me tell you that after passing my High School examination with good marks, I got some financial help from a kind gentleman and eventually did M.B.A. Seeing the booming business in the real estate, I tried my hands at it and with your good luck image of Lakshmi, I succeeded and began to purchase many properties. I saw your name which I remembered well from my student days and immediately took it to the court to pay back your kind gesture in the best possible manner I could."

❖❖❖

15

THE RECONCILIATOR

Creative writing is undoubtedly a pleasurable activity in which a person gets so much immersed that he forgets everything including himself and that is where for him all the problems begin. Quite a few things were already bothering me, such as, terrorism in Punjab and the safety of Hindus, but the immediate one was from my wife Surmai Mathur.

During the 1980's and 1990's, the Punjab had the daily killings of three-dozen Hindus at the hands of terrorists. Hence one had to observe voluntary curfew hours not to move out from dusk to dawn and to remain confined to the four walls of the residence. Being a university teacher, I remained largely confined to my room, reading, writing and watching television. For my family's safety, I had taken a licensed revolver which gave me some courage at such times.

I had the habit of writing critical as well as creative writing in my bed room. Unless I lay down comfortably on my bed, my vision did not get fully activated. It was like a water hose with low pressure which slowed down the flow of water on a certain height but ran smoothly in a horizontal position. The moment I lay down on the bed, the ideas and corresponding words flowed smoothly and by turning to my side, I would either write down smoothly with a pen or would correct my earlier draft for better and more appropriate expressions.

This is where the problem would begin. While lying down on one side of the bed, the other side would be occupied by some sheets of paper, a pocket dictionary, and a few books for my teaching job in the university at Amritsar. The result would be that the double-bed meant for me and my wife would have absolutely no place for her which naturally made her often infuriated, saying, "You should have got married with your books rather than with me. They are all over the bed, leaving no place for me."

For a number of days, I bore this frequently-repeated harangue as a sort of daily ritual, like a few of them in the Hindu religion; you could only wait for them to be over. Our choices were limited because only the two of us were there in the house; our children having been in jobs in Bombay. Whether we lived well or quarreled, we had to live together.

One night, there was really no room on the entire bed for her as my books and papers were spread out all over it. Surmai Mathur, my wife, must have been tired or had some unpleasant exchanges with the maid servant and hence came in a very angry mood, saying, "Your books are my *sautan* – co-wife. Today either they or I am going to be there on the bed" and saying this, she began to throw my books on the ground. Since some of my books and journals were kept open for cross-references for a research paper, I asked her to wait for a moment so that I could place some book markers before closing them but she was prepared to listen not even a word from me.

Even though I was also angry that she could not wait for me to place markers in books before closing them, I remained rather cool – two angry beings under the same roof could have been devastatingly tragic. Picking up all my books and papers, I shifted to the second room and began to work there. We had our silent dinner and instead of sleeping in the same room, we slept in different rooms.

For two or three days, our cold war continued. She cooked meals, served them, and both of us ate at the same table without exchanging a word. On the fourth day in the afternoon, I found her silent in the kitchen. Though I had a mind to go and comfort her but on such occasions in the past, her reactions had been violent and I refrained from it.

One week passed this way. Like the international cold war, we remained two separate entities in seemingly harmonious relationship. Whenever the visitors came, we behaved as though nothing had happened, but our cold war was resumed the moment they left the place.

Some people have anxiously prying eyes and could surmise that below the tranquil relationship, something cranky existed which none of us was prepared to divulge. When my closest friend Brahma Deep came, he talked about the killings of Hindus on that particular day and cautioned me against such a danger.

I assured him, "I keep a loaded licensed revolver for prompt use in such a situation. That is all one can do."

Brahma Deep then attempted to be a negotiator between the two of us but he failed. My wife Surmai was too obstinate to budge an inch from her stand that either she or my books will be there on her side of the bed; whereas I could do nothing without either of them. As a temporary reconciliation, I had already shifted to the room meant for guests and that is what I had become.

We met silently at the dining table three times a day – for breakfast, lunch and dinner. We took care that we did not speak with each other. I remember that in Tulsidas's *Ram Charita Manas,* Ram, under the agony of Sita's separation, would ask the trees and animals about Sita's whereabouts. Similarly, we, instead of conversing directly with each other, assumed our absence and talked with walls, doors or windows, and that too in a telegraphic language as if each word, like in a telegram, were to cost a fortune. I would say, "Curtain ji, what vegetable curry today?"

Surmai would say, "Window ji, potato and tomato."

Sometimes, she would chant couplets like this in a sing-song way:

"None talks to me and I talk to none;
Meals on the table; may take anyone."

There was no question of touching each other as if one of us were an untouchable. When my friend wanted both of us to shake hands, we moved our heads in the negative.

Gradually, the rumours about our cold war found their way among some common friends of ours who looked at each of us with mysterious smiles and suspicious eyes. One of them asked me, "How long?" implying thereby how long the quarrel has gone on?

I replied, "It is the beginning of the second glorious week," recalling the terminology used for the running period of a movie in a particular theatre of the city.

Once my next door neighbour came and, suspecting something not quite normal, asked me, "Both of you must show maturity and start talking. The silence in your house upsets us too."

I laughed, "Sir, we never quarreled so vociferously as to make it an audible radio programme for neighbors."

He asked, "Aniket, we heard that you people don't touch each other. Is it true?"

"It is true, sir, because both of us happen to be divinely blessed people," I explained. "Like the mythic King Midas, she has been blessed with a boon that whatever she touches will be transformed into gold and she does not want that to happen to me. Similarly, I have been blessed with a boon that whatever I, like Bhasmasur, touch will be reduced to ashes. Hence we refrain from touching each other."

"Professor Aniket Mathur ji," my neighbor said with a glint in his eyes. "I know very well that you are a learned professor and can deflect any question to some obscure allusions which I can neither understand nor dispute. My simple question is: are there any chances of reconciliation and compromise between the two?"

"Not that I know of in very near future," I said.

"Okay," he said. "Being a neighbor and well-wisher, I thought I should try, though I am sure soon everything will be alright."

Hearing of our cold war, my eldest sister Ratna came in quite a threatening mood and badly scolded me, "Aniket, I cannot say much to Surmai, because she has come from outside of our family and there is none else other than you to give her a psychological support. But Aniket, you are my younger brother and I am going to thrash you in public place in order to force a compromise between the two of you. Out of my experience as a woman, I know it well that if any of you simply hugs the other one warmly, the ice will be broken and rapprochement reached. Would you like to do it now?"

I smiled, touched her feet, folded my hands and said, "You are quite right Didi. Give us some more time. Have no fear, we are not going to go in for divorce. I assure you that within a week or so, everything will be alright."

"Okay," Ratna felt convinced. "I believe, you have seen the movie 'Munna Bhai M.B.B.S.' wherein Munna Bhai transforms the entire atmosphere of the hospital so much merely by his act of liberally giving a *jhappi* – a crushing embrace – to any one that all the people from the sweeper to the doctors came in his support, defying the highest authority. If you don't patch up, Aniket, within the next ten days, I'll thrash you openly outside your house so that everyone notices the thrashing of a university teacher."

What she had said was true but a crushing embrace by any of us at an inappropriate time is like giving rich food to an anemic patient who has neither hunger nor inclination for it. I thought that what my sister had said was true because at the time of Holi festivities, a warm hug brings even enemies together. The parting hugs to the newly-married, departing girl and the mother's embraces of the crying child were good examples before me.

Hardly had my elder sister gone when a powerful, ear-piercing shriek from Surmai made me suspect that some terrorist had either threatened her from outside or had made a forced entry into the kitchen. Taking my revolver, I rushed towards the kitchen but midway, Surmai met and hugged me with such a forceful impact that I nearly fell backwards. If she had her way, it appeared, she would have hidden herself into my lap. It was definite now that some terrorist must have attempted to intrude into the kitchen or she would not have come that way.

I yelled at her, "Surmai, what's the matter?"

Terribly shaken to death, she held her head and face partly covered with both hands. Her eyes were still closed and she refused to open them; instead, clutching at my clothes with her left hand, she directed me with her right hand towards the kitchen.

Patting her head and back, I hurriedly smoothened her ruffled feathers, and then tearing her away from me, I rushed to the kitchen. Moving the revolver in all directions of the kitchen and glancing with searching eyes everywhere, I found none. The wire-mesh kitchen door was bolted from inside which meant that the terrorist had not entered the kitchen.

By this time, Surmai had followed me behind in the kitchen and I asked her, "Where... who is there? I find none here."

She pointed out at the floor where a giant cockroach was moving its antennas and near-popping eyes around threatening none in particular.

I exclaimed, "cockroach?"

She clutched at my back, pleading pathetically, "Don't leave me alone, Aniket. I am mortally afraid of it and cannot do without you."

❖❖❖

16

BLESSED BE THE DARK

There was time when Prashant Talwar was a great lover of beautiful women, particularly very fair complexioned, but now a very attractive, pretty woman does not mean someone pleasing, tempting, giving ecstatic pleasure, but an embodied danger. When he sees one, a sense of fear begins to creep upon him, a giant shadow inching every moment towards him. She appears a tempting disaster, a wonderful mirage, an embodied inner death, someone to be avoided like a corona-infected person. Such a feeling has made him nervous and fearful. It has altogether changed his attitude to life.

Mahasweta, as her name suggested, was an extremely fair complexioned and the most beautiful girl of the Holkar College, Indore. She was in MBA first year and happened to be Prashant's class fellow. Most students of the college hovered over her, attempting to draw a sentence, a word or even a smiling look from her but she disappointed them. Prashant Talwar, though gifted with an extremely handsome personality, was interested in studies and hence remained detached from such activities. Coming from a middle class family, he wanted to have a high percentage of marks for a good job so that he could shoulder the burden of his parental family.

He was sitting in the library of the college, when someone cooed, "Prashant, how come you are studying here whereas most students are watching the cricket match! Would you like to accompany me there?"

He looked at Mahasweta in surprise. She was talking to him on her own when he had not even wished her, but seeing her beauty, Prashant, mesmerised by the offer, closed the book and accompanied her to the cricket ground.

Prashant's mother had once casually told him that his love for the fair-complexioned beauty was ingrained in him from his very childhood. When he was five-year old, he would gradually gravitate towards the most beautiful woman, gaze and smile at her till she would hold his finger, kiss him or place him in her lap. Hence his mother was exhilarated when his college affair with Mahasweta – a paragon of beauty – got converted into a matrimonial alliance. Unfortunately, after a couple of years of Mahasweta's death, his mother was disappointed, even terribly frustrated by his second marriage with Shyama who was of pitch dark complexion! And the mother was not alone.

One of his friends, who had seen his fair-complexioned wife Mahasweta earlier, asked Prashant in surprise at his dark coloured wife Shyama now, "Where did you have Bhabhi ji dyed?"

"At Bombay Dyeing," Prashant smilingly replied.

When Shyama was kneading the flour, a relation from the countryside asked her, "You don't knead the flour."

"Why?"

"The dark colour of your hand might leave a shade of it on the dough."

Shyama was quick to respond in an equally stringent tone: "Did Mahasweta make the dough white while kneading it? With the touch of her hands, it might have become as white as the wet chalk powder!"

It silenced the woman but not every mouth could be shut.

One day when Shyama was washing her hands with a soap, another woman said, "You are wasting the soap for nothing."

"Why?"

"No matter how much soap you apply, the black color of your hands would not go. A mountain of soaps cannot whiten a crow."

After bearing such humiliations stoically for a long time, Shyama wished never to be pregnant for fears of producing a similar child. Much against her wishes, when she did become pregnant, shivers ran down her spine on realisation that if a daughter happened to be born with her traits and complexion rather than with those of her handsome husband, it would be the duplication of her misfortunes. And her fears turned out to be true. She gave birth to a daughter as dark as she herself was. She cried incessantly for days and nights.

On the frequent eruption of Shyama's cries, Prashant asked, "It is surprising that you are crying so much over her dark complexion when you yourself have it!"

Wiping off her tears, Shyama said, "Since I have suffered so intensely due to dark complexion, I never wanted my daughter Jeena to go through the same torture. Believe me, Prashant, I was so much anguished by her birth that at one time I wanted to kill her by throttling her neck. How can I forget that my whole life has been a long tale of sufferings from taunts and derisive comments? But it seems as if god has shaped my daughter from the same lump of clay left over after making me."

Prashant consoled her, "In a way, the dark complexion has an in-built safety. Atleast she would not have an acid attack as Mahasweta had."

After cooling down a little, Shyama asked him, "You always avoided telling me why she was attacked with acid and by whom. Tell me the reason at least now."

"It is a long story, Shyama," Prashant said with a deep sigh. "Mahasweta was so exceedingly beautiful that many one-sided lovers wanted to marry or at least to befriend her. Some people often harassed her on different occasions. They would pass dirty comments on her way to or from the college. Of course, she was quite frank and fearless. One day, a person looking at her loudly said, 'The moon comes up in the night. How come it has appeared during day time?' and laughed loudly. Mahasweta yelled back, 'The owl comes out in the night. How come it has shown its ominous face during daytime today?' Such retaliatory responses antagonised these boys much more and they openly swore of teaching her a lesson. When my marriage was fixed with her, one of them threatened her many times not to marry me or else either of us would be killed. Once there was a fatal attack on me but I escaped. Unfortunately, someone in my absence poured the entire can of acid on her. She had 75 percent burns on her body. Her sufferings before death were so painful, so terrible, so nerve-wrecking that everyone in the hospital wished even for her death to save her at least from her heart-rending cries of pain. On that day, I had decided never to marry such a beautiful woman again."

So this was the reason, Shyama realised, that Prashant had married her despite her dark complexion. Now what will he do when his dark-complelxioned daughter suffers? When their daughter Jeena had grown up a little and had begun to have consciousness of dark complexion, Shyama advised, "Jeena, my daughter, I'll not let you suffer because of your complexion. I shall remain your shield like the protective armors of mythical Karna with which he was born."

Jeena took to heart her mother's advice of not taking things lying down which used to cause her inner sufferings but at the same time not to retaliate brutally which would create enemies for her but to set an example of stoicism before others so that people looked at her as an exemplary person who could transcend physical handicaps to attain something great.

With Shyama's encouragement and coaxing, Jeena became so inwardly preoccupied with a visionary light that the taunts and teasing remarks of the class fellows disturbed her but only momentarily. She remained like a proverbial pillar of transcendental peace.

One day, a class fellow shamelessly asked, "Why is your complexion so dark?"

It was a point-blank question which straightway hit her heart like a dart on the target. She was so puzzled she did not know how to respond and said, "Is that how you feel? I never see myself that way." When the boy went on staring at her, Jeena said in a somewhat cool manner, "My dear friend, it is nature's gift. Did you ever ask why the crow was so dark, or the swan so white or the rainbow had seven different colours? It is all the fecundity of nature."

Driven partly by her inferiority complex and partly due to her inner desire to shine or even outshine others in studies, Jeena worked very hard. Consequently, both parents and teachers were surprised when they found her always maintaining the first position in different classes.

Once a debate was organised in the school on the problem of colour consciousness in India and Jeena spoke extremely well against colour discrimination. Her speech was so impassioned, so well arranged and argued so logically and convincingly that the three judges unanimously gave a verdict that Jeena was undoubtedly a gifted child who must be encouraged to do something great and to bring a good name to the area. One of them thought that her words were so well chosen, so appropriate and so forceful as if Saraswati herself were sitting on her tongue.

Bathing in the glory of laudatory comments, Jeena for the first time realised that her dark complexion was not really that dark and occasionally had a flitting feeling that probably it was better so. However, in lonely hours, her mind remained preoccupied with the unpleasantness connected with the dark colour. Why did God drape her in this colour? If her physical features were so beautiful, so picturesque, so well-chiseled as she noticed herself, why did god give her the unpleasant colour? Such a feeling made her angry and she spoke unpleasantly to others, though repented afterwards.

When her one fair-complexioned girlfriend wished to shake hand with Jeena, the latter said, "Are you sure, my fairy, that it would not make your hand dirty by its contact with my black hand?"

The girl friend smiled at her response and said, "Jeena, you are right. Since my tainted hand alone would look odd, I would like to have my whole body disfigured by hugging you." And she embraced Jeena so warmly, so lovingly that the latter felt exhilarated and yet ashamed and apologetic for having used such caustic words.

In the night, Jeena coolly contemplated and realised that if such an enviously beautiful girl could be so disarmingly sweet and courteous in her talk and behaviour with her, she too must learn not to use barbed words for anyone. Even with her dark complexion, she could be warm and loving to those who were not antagonistic to her. That way, her words could endear her to others even when her dark complexion made her unattractive, if not repulsive.

Having enjoyed the best literary works in Hindi and English both in B.A. and M.A., Jeena many times pondered over their beautiful passages and wished she could write such pieces. She memorised quotable lines of literary excellence and munched them over and over again as they yielded deep, hidden meanings. A simple couplet explained that a cuckoo and a crow had the same black colour but whereas the former's melodious voice attracted the people, the latter's raucous cries drew stones. She internalised the example and thought to keep it in mind particularly while dealing with others..

No matter how much Jeena tried to remain cheerful by pushing the colour consciousness away from her, she could not totally escape from being brooding and introvert. She had her own room and often worked on her laptop. Though as a father, Prashant was supposed to keep an eye over her activities, he never asked her what work she did, nor did she ever tell him about it. He remained happy in her happiness.

Once Prashant was surprised when his colleague in the bank talked about an article in an English newspaper under Jeena Talwar's name and he wondered whether it was by his daughter! When she confirmed that the article was by her, he was very happy. He was all the more surprised when she told him that her other articles too had appeared in the newspaper earlier.

"But you never told me about it Jeena?" he asked in surprise.

"Father, it is not something great," Jeena explained. "What I write is merely a fraction of my inner feelings; these essays are somewhat purgatory, unburdening of my soul. Such confessional writings give me a lot of relief by releasing the ever-building pressure within me and in castigating the society which continues to champion the monster of Indian apartheid."

Prashant read her essay minutely and was impressed particularly by two things: the genuineness of her feelings and the felicity of her expression. Inwardly, he found in her a pronounced potentiality of a writer. What relieved him was that the dark complexion instead of making her psychic was breeding in her a desire to fight, a ferocious soldier armed merely with the pen as a weapon.

One day Prashant had the greatest surprise of his life when he read the news item that Jeena Talwar's debut novel *Blessed be the Dark* has been published in the U.K. and short listed for Booker Prize for portraying so graphically, so minutely the consciousness of dark complexion among Indian girls.

Prashant rushed to her in the kitchen and read the news item. "Jeena," he said in a bubbling, jubilant voice. "You have been short listed for the Booker Prize of this year."

"What for?" she coolly yet with a tinge of mischief asked.

"For your debut novel."

"Is that so?" she asked in a rather casual way, preparing breakfast for him.

"Are you not excited? Not surprised?" Prashant asked her.

Without showing any emotion, she said, “May be! May not be!”

He was rather taken aback that Jeena was taking such a great piece of news so lightly without any excitement. Seeing him in such a state, she coolly said, “Father, I had the information beforehand.”

“Why didn’t you tell me about it?” he asked.

“I call you, father, for breakfast only when it is fully prepared, not when it is still in the process.”

❖❖❖

17

REVERSAL

An old widow is like an antiquated brass utensil, once of high value now being discarded for new wares. Tejaswani was a 60-year old widow who stayed in the house with her son Mithalesh and his wife Pinky. Both of them worked in different offices. Despite double salaries, they perpetually grumbled at the rising cost of living.

To them, Tejaswani was an undesirable member but for her family pension, a major part of which was always spent in grocery and vegetables. No matter how much she gave them, the couple always remained crossed with her. Despite doing all sorts of house management chores, Tejaswani never heard a word of praise from them. Their daughter Samita, however, was intimately attached with her. In her childhood, she would come to the grandmother after taking evening meals, and listen to interesting tales from the *Ramayana*, the *Mahabharata* and *Panchatantra* before going to sleep.

Now Samita was eighteen years old. Sometimes, she would sit with her grandmother to see what her steel box contained. Tejaswani would show her old bridal ornaments – exquisite nose ring (*nath*), earrings, necklaces with diamond pendants, golden armlets, gold bangles – broad and thin ones, silver waist belt with peacock patterns, and rings with silver chains for all fingers of both hands, anklets and many more. Tejaswani assured

Samita that all those ornaments would be given away to her in her marriage since they are of no use to her.

"But Dadi Ma, they are very old. They are not in fashion now."

"Those which are outdated will be sold or exchanged for new ones," Tejaswani explained, "Gold and silver always remain valuable."

Tejaswani was very active as the Sports teacher in a Girls' college. Though the age of retirement was sixty, Tejaswani had sought a voluntary retirement at fifty-five because her husband was suffering from blood cancer in the last stage. After his death, she decided to divert her attention to the house management in order to give relief to her working daughter-in-law, but she found out that no matter how much she did in the house, Pinky always remained sour-faced with her.

On one Sunday, Samita took her grandmother to the park. They came across Tejaswani's former boss Mayank Raj of the Sports Department of Gorakhpur University. During the Sports weeks in the university, she used to take her team to his university where he was the Director as well as the Coordinator of Sports activities. Most of the time, Tejaswani's college team among girls used to have the first, second or third rank and he used to praise her work profusely in glowing terms. She was all the more surprised to see him in Allahabad because he used to be in Gorakhpur.

After wishing him, Tejaswani expressed surprise, "Sir, how come you are in Allahabad? You used to be in Gorakhpur."

"How come you are in Allahabad, Tejaswani? You used to be in Mau College."

Tejaswani found him the same cheerful person he used to be in Gorakhpur. Mayank Raj seemed happy to see her after nearly five years. He said, "I was working in Gorakhpur but I belong to Allahabad. I have my own house here. Since my son's family is in Calcutta, I am alone here. My wife passed away three years ago. My house is very close to the park and I come here every morning. Two things attract me to this place: very fresh air and the company of green trees all-around."

"Which means you don't like our company," Tejaswani laughed.

"No, your company too is most welcome."

Introducing Samita to him, Tejaswani said, "She is Samita, my granddaughter. It is she who has brought me to the park; otherwise my son and daughter-in-law are against it."

Samita said to him, "Uncle, the hesitation she has is that being a widow, she would be criticized by people."

"I am surprised," he said to Tejaswani, "that you have been in the Sports department for so many years but still harbour such ideas!"

"It is not my view," Tejaswani said to him. "Others may say vulgar or scandalous things which might reach my son and his wife and they don't like such things. Being in Sports department all my life, I have lived among people and hence isolation in any form terrifies me to death."

Since Mayank Raj was meeting her after a long time, he brought three cups of tea. As they began to sip it, Tejaswani laughed loudly. Mayank Raj thought she was laughing at him and somewhat upset, he began to adjust his clothes, his hair, and then she said, "It is nothing to do with you, sir. Your cup of tea reminded me of an incident."

"What is it?" he asked.

"Nothing significant," she said.

"Please Tejaswani, do tell us. In Gorakhpur, you used to tell your husband's forgetful habits which were very humorous."

"Alright, Sir," she said. "My husband used to have a cup of hot water for his shave every morning. After he had shaved his beard, he said to me, 'Today the shaving hot water was very dirty.' "

"But I haven't given hot water for shave yet," she had said in surprise.

"Then what was it?"

"I had given you a cup of hot tea which you have used as shaving water."

While Tejaswani, Samita and Mayank Raj were laughing, she noticed that Mithalesh and Pinky were passing by from the place, looking somewhat cross at her. When they reached home, Mithalesh asked her, "Mother, who was with you and Samita laughing in the park?"

She said, "He was Mayank Raj – a retired Director of Sports from Gorakhpur University under whom I was working in Mau college."

On that day, no one talked with Tejaswani. The faces of her son and his wife were gloomy and morose. Many times Tejaswani felt so depressed by their behaviour that she thought of the futility of living with them. The only person who took her good care was Samita. Now she was going to go to the Medical College, Benares. A month before her departure, Samita took her to the park almost every day. Sometimes they sat with

Mayank Raj but most of the time he was seen going with other men, laughing or talking with them.

When all three were sitting together in the park, Samita persuaded her Dadi Ma to tell the best incident of her husband's forgetfulness and it was supported by Mayank Raj.

"Samita," Tejaswani began, "Your grandfather was not really that forgetful. As a Professor of Physics, he had contributed the largest number of research papers in physics in the entire government college. Since his mind was always preoccupied with some problem or other of physics, he did not while away his time in other things. Hence he had never gone to see a movie but one day I and your father Mithalesh, when he was young, forced him to accompany us to see a movie in a theatre. As the movie began, he was turning and twisting in his seat. After sometime, he got up and left the hall never to return again."

After a brief pause, she continued, "When we reached home, we found him sitting on the *chabootara* – platform in front of the house, waiting for us. The moment we reached, he was very angry, saying, 'Where had you people gone? I have been waiting for you people for two hours. You did not even leave the keys or any message with neighbors.'"

"After listening to his angry outburst, Mithalesh and I had a hearty laugh which further infuriated him and he said, "'All of you are laughing! Where had you gone?'"

"To see a movie."

"With whom?"

"With you," Mithalesh and I had said and everyone laughed again.

Samita said, "Dadi Ma, you have such wonderfully pleasant memories. If you just remember them, your loneliness would go away."

Tejaswani explained, "Such things come to the mind, Samita, only when one happens to be in a good company or mood. Today we had such a good time, but let us see, Samita, what happens today at home because your parents were passing by when we were laughing."

When they reached home, Mithalesh straightway asked in anger, "Mother, you were laughing loudly again with that Kalank Raj."

"Mayank Raj," she corrected.

"Whatever be the name. If you like him, do anything with him but do not take my daughter with you. I don't want her to be defamed. We have been hearing loose talk about your association with male members but did not believe till today when we saw ourselves how shamelessly you were indulging in loud guffaws with an unknown man."

"He is not an unknown man," she replied. "I worked under him in Gorakhpur University. We worked that way for 20 years. My husband never objected to it."

"Alright," he said, "within a couple of days we shall be leaving for Bombay for two months. You can do anything you like during that period."

Tejaswani was very unhappy and cried in a corner by closing the door of her room. She recalled how her husband used to encourage her for such outings. After his death, she had become a working machine confined to a corner of the house where her boredom was relieved only occasionally by her granddaughter.

On their official work tour, Mithalesh left for Bombay accompanied by his wife for two months, leaving her and Samita at home. The latter went to Benares, leaving her grandmother alone. Before leaving for Benares, she requested Mayank Raj, "Please take care of my grandmother who is all alone. I have taken a promise from her that she would go to the park everyday. Of course, I will call her everyday."

One day when Samita called her grandmother, there was no response. She might have gone somewhere, she thought. The next day, she made many calls at different times but there was no response, though rings were going on quite clearly.

Now Samita was worried and imagined many horrifying possibilities. She called Mayank Raj and said, "Uncle, please go to my house and check my grandmother. She has not been responding for the last two days. Hope she is not ill."

Mayank Raj went to the house and found Tejaswani in high fever. She had taken no medicine. Her body was burning. He called the physician who prescribed some medicines which were to be taken at short intervals.

Since there was no one else to give her medicine, Mayank Raj in consultation with Samita shifted her to his house. He took her good care for seven days and nights till she recovered completely from severe case of typhoid. When Samita came, she expressed her gratitude to Mayank Raj. He said, "Since you had given me the responsibility, it was my moral duty to take care of her. Now that you have come, she can be shifted to your house."

"But I want you to visit us regularly because there is the psychological part of illness too. She must have found in you a person with whom she could easily discuss her problems."

"There is no problem in visiting your place," Mayank Raj said, "but your parents, on their arrival, might create a hell for her. You know they have already objected to her meeting me even in your presence."

Samita thought for sometime and taking him to a different room, she said, "I want to discuss something very confidential with you. I saw my grandmother when she was working in a college and now when she is confined to the house. As a matter of fact, she must be feeling suffocation in our house. My parents are very self-centred and are concerned with her pension and the work in the house. As a matter of fact, had you not taken care of her in my absence, she could have succumbed to her illness."

Mayank Raj said, "I did what I could and I am happy about it."

"I have been thinking over this problem for more than a month in order to find a lasting solution." Samita said. "She can't remain in a separate room by herself as we have seen what happened to her during her illness. Her life at our place is a virtual hell. I have found a solution which depends wholly on your cooperation and help."

"I'll be glad to do what I can," he said.

"Could you do one thing?" Samita earnestly pleaded. "You are alone and so is she. Both of you like each other. My feeling is: could it not be converted into a matrimonial relationship?"

Mayank Raj looked at Samita in utter surprise. It was unbelievable for him to visualise a granddaughter arranging a match for her grandmother. Wondering whether the proposal had come as a mockery to characterise their relationship or was a genuine suggestion of a well-wisher, he asked her, "Are you serious?"

"Nothing but serious, Uncle ji," she said. "I have seen faces of both of you when you are together and the pathetic face of my grandmother in our house."

"What is to be done?" he asked.

She said, "You are an experienced person equivalent to my late grandfather. If you agree with my suggestion, you take her out and persuade her for marriage. The rest we can finalise."

It was not quite easy for Tejaswani to think of remarriage at the age of sixty. Everyone in the house and in the neighborhood was likely to make fun of her. Some of them might say that her body had so much of fire that it could not be quenched in sixty years by her husband and hence is getting ready to have another thrasher, not knowing at all that it is the company one seeks in the old age.

Realising the painful period of widowhood after her husband's death, her recent illness and Mayank Raj's care, and the possibility of ill-treatment after the return of her son and his wife, she, with a great deal of hesitation, gave her consent.

Afterwards, Mayank Raj and Samita made other preparations, arranged two witnesses and got married in the court.

In the evening, as a small gathering was arranged in a hotel, Samita made her Dadi Ma wear all those ornaments which she had kept reserved for her marriage. Accepting felicitations from all, Tejaswani hugged Samita and said, "I used to talk often of arranging Samita's marriage and had reserved all these ornaments for her marriage, but she has reversed the role by doing it for me."

❖❖❖

18

A MAN OF GOLD

It pained Vipul Asthana that despite his earnest desire, he could do nothing to help his childhood friend Ghasi Ram Swarnakar. Vipul considered the latter a man of gold who had helped him many times and had even saved his life in his childhood. He attempted to persuade Ghasi Ram in many ways to accept some help but he failed. The man had so much of self-respect that he did not want to accept any help from his childhood friend.

Ghasi Ram Swarnakar and Vipul Asthana belonged to Danpur village and studied together in Junior High School, Pehroni. They stayed in a dormitory. Pehroni was nine miles away from Danpur village. Since the road to Pehroni was a mere dirt road, both of them went on foot on Mondays and came back home on Saturdays.

Ghasi Ram's father was the richest goldsmith in the area. He had a large house with a number of milch cattle heads. In his neighborhood, there was a wrestling arena where Ghasi Ram did physical exercises and consumed a lot of milk, ghee and dry fruits. Naturally his physique was like that of a young wrestler.

Vipul Asthana, on the other hand, was the son of an honest Patwari Rama Nand who did not have much money. He was lean and thin and somewhat incapable of doing hard physical work. On way to Pehroni, whenever Vipul's legs were caught in the muddy road and he was unable to extricate them himself,

Ghasi Ram pulled them out. However, the latter was quite weak in his studies and hence Vipul helped him in his homework. This way, their friendship continued.

Though Vipul's bags were carried by Ghasi Ram in the journey, Vipul felt it very difficult to cover the distance of nine miles on foot and would need to take rest at every milestone. As a consequence, the normal three-hour journey from Danpur to Pehroni began for them in the morning and came to an end only in the evening.

Ghasi Ram was somewhat religious minded and believed in god. Being very tired, Vipul sat down on the bare ground and pathetically whined, "Ghasi Ram, I am dead tired though we still have four miles to go. Since you believe in God, please ask Him to shorten the distance to Pehroni from 4 to 2 or even 1 mile."

Laughing loudly, Ghasi Ram made fun of Vipul and said, "Why don't you go and sit in your mother's lap? God never reduces such distances. Instead, now that the road is a little better, we can pray for a bullock cart in which we can ask for a ride for you."

Vipul asked, "Do you believe a bullock cart may come?"

Ghasi Ram laughed, "A bullock cart is not going to descend here from the sky but a good possibility is there that if a bullock cart happens to come this way, you may seek a ride."

After sometime, a bullock cart did come from Danpur side which was obviously going to Pehroni. Ghasi Ram asked the cart man, "Brother, this boy cannot walk on this rough, semi-dry, mud road. Could you give him a ride?" When the cart man hesitated, Ghasi Ram added, "He is the son of Patwari Rama Nand."

"Is that so?" the cart man stopped his cart immediately, saying, "Rama Nand has been like a god to me. He helped me many times." Motioning Vipul to take a seat in the cart, he asked Ghasi Ram, "And who is your father?"

"Radhey Shyam Swarnakar."

Calling Ghasi Ram, he said, "You too can sit in the cart, though your father had cheated me once by mixing some alloy with the gold I had given for two earrings for my wife." Giggling humorously, he added, "It is said that a goldsmith adulterates gold even if it belongs to his sister. Isn't it true Ghasi Ram?" Ghasi Ram, however, remained silent

At the end of the year, Ghasi Ram had failed his 8th class examination while Vipul, after passing it, went for further studies.

❖❖❖

Many years passed. Ghasi Ram was now 30 years old, managing the shop after the death of his father. The traditional customers continued to come to him and his business went on in a normal way.

In 1968, the Government of India passed the Gold Control Order in which several restrictions were imposed on the processing of gold. No unlicensed goldsmiths were permitted to make gold ornaments. It was also not easy to get a license and, as a result, most goldsmiths were ruined. Silver ornaments alone did not fetch sufficient money. The thriving business of Ghasi Ram suffered a terrible setback. The luxurious life which the family was leading since his father's time now came to an end.

Meanwhile, Vipul had passed his M.Sc. examination, had successfully competed for I.P.S. and had become now the Superintendent of Police in the State of Maharashtra. Once in a while, he visited his Danpur village and met Ghasi Ram whose business was running in a mere skeletal form.

When Vipul went to Ghasi Ram, they exchanged their memories of childhood. Ghasi Ram reminded Vipul, "You wanted to become a Police Officer and now you have become one."

"You are better off too Ghasi Ram," Vipul laughed. "You wanted to become a giraffe and are a man of gold now."

"Is that right?" Kalpana, Ghasi Ram's wife, asked in surprise. "I never heard of it. Why did he want to become a giraffe?"

Much to the embarrassment of Kalpana, Vipul went over the past and narrated the incident, "In our school days, the most dreaded period was that of English. The English teacher used to ask meanings and spellings of difficult English words which was quite a tough job for Ghasi Ram, though not so difficult for me. When the teacher asked Ghasi Ram the meaning of any difficult word, I helped him by whispering at his back but many times all my efforts failed and he had to face punishment."

After taking a long breath, Vipul continued, "Since Ghasi Ram was rather healthy, the punishment was to be proportionately harsher than that of others. Taking a fresh sapling of *Kaner* – oleander tree and stripping it of its leaves, he would strike Ghasi Ram's palms so forcefully that it would leave purple marks on them. Many times, the teacher devised other methods. Along with slapping his puffed up cheeks, he demanded a couple of pebbles one each of which would be placed on two earlobes and pressed hard with thumb and forefinger which must have been so excruciatingly painful that Ghasi Ram cried and that brought a fiendish smile of satisfaction on the teacher's face as if the tears were a mark of the latter's success."

Kalpana looked at her husband who nodded his head to say it was so. Vipul proceeded, "Once on the occasion of Holi, all the teachers and students attended the function in which they expressed their views somewhat freely. The main question was: what would you like to be in the future or in the next life? What some of them preferred were: a king, the President or Prime Minister of India, a lion, a rich man's dog, among others. I expressed my desire to be a Police Officer. Ghasi Ram said, 'I would like to be a giraffe?' Disbelieving his choice, the teacher asked. 'What! Why such a strange choice like a giraffe?' Ghasi Ram explained, 'So that no teacher could punish me by slapping me or pinching my earlobes with pebbles.'"

Vipul, Kalpana and Ghasi Ram laughed vigorously.

In his subsequent visit when Vipul met Ghasi Ram, the latter told him about his agricultural land which was encroached upon by a village Thakur. Vipul met his counterpart in the city of Nanitpur who ordered the Tehsildar of Pehroni and everything was settled within two days. The markers were fixed on the boundary of his land so that none could encroach again in the future. The Thakur was also warned that any further mischief would land him in jail.

After everything was done, Vipul went to Ghasi Ram's house. Both he and his wife were immensely grateful and thanked him profusely by folding their hands. Seeing that his wife had only glass bangles in her hands, Vipul asked, "Bhabhi ji, you belong to the goldsmith family but how come you don't have gold bangles in your hands?"

Kalpana said, "They were given to me in marriage but had to be sold for the treatment of our elder son. Now only god knows when the chance would come again."

Vipul said, "Two bangles now cost only around twenty to thirty thousand rupees. I am ready to give that much money now. It can be taken as a gift of a friend."

"No, no, no," Ghasi Ram vigorously moved his hands. "I cannot accept it. You have already done enough for me."

"Bhabhi ji," Vipul said. "Ghasi Ram had saved my life once. But for him, I would have died on that day. Didn't he tell you about it?"

"No," she said. "When was it?"

Vipul recounted the past: "In our childhood days, on one Monday, as Ghasi Ram and I had covered some distance on way to Pehroni, it had begun to rain heavily. When we reached the river, it was overflowing the low-level bridge. Even though it was only ankle-deep water on the bridge, I was badly scared by seeing the sea of muddy water all around. I did not want to go further. Since we were in the middle of the bridge, going back was as risky as going forward. Ghasi Ram took our bags over his one shoulder, held my hand in the other and proceeded to cross the flooded river chanting loudly "Jai Shri Ram" and "Jai Hanuman." I moved very slowly, planting each of my feet firmly, but at one place, they began to lose their grip and I began to cry, saying, 'Ghasi Ram, my feet cannot hold the ground. I don't want to go further. It seems I am going to die. Please save me.'"

Vipul felt ashamed of his own weakness while Kalpana and Ghasi Ram laughed. He continued, "Ghasi Ram assured me not to have fear and that before my death, he would die first. He made me sit astride his neck with both my feet hanging on both sides. When we reached the other end of the river, both of us felt relieved."

Taking a long breath, Vipul said, "Now tell me Bhabhi ji, what are gold bangles before his act of saving my life?"

Kalpana kept quiet but Ghasi Ram said, "I won't accept them."

"Then take money for it as a loan," Vipul persuaded, "and you can pay me back in installments."

"No," Ghasi Ram asserted. "That is also not desirable. Taking loan for wife's bangles would make me a laughing stock in the village."

"People say," Vipul said in a low voice, "that goldsmiths always pilfer some gold from each ornament they make. Can't you do that for Bhabhi ji's bangles?"

Ghasi Ram giggled in a suppressed way, saying, "First of all, now no customers come openly for having their gold ornaments made because there is no license-holding goldsmith in Danpur village. And if someone does bring some gold, a goldsmith can barely pilfer less than one-fourth of a gram per ten grams of gold whereas for bangles, 20 to 30 grams of gold is needed."

"Tell me one more thing, Ghasi Ram," Vipul anxiously asked. "Can a goldsmith pilfer gold when people get their ornaments prepared at their own homes?"

Now Ghasi Ram was freer as if a student were being asked a very simple question. He laughed again and said, "That much trick a goldsmith learns from his childhood. They are known to steal collyrium from a lady's eyes!"

"Ghasi Ram," Vipul said very mildly but forcefully. "Tomorrow, I shall bring three gold coins of 10 grams each for two bangles. You will have to make them in my house. If you succeed in adulterating them with some alloy, the bangles would be yours for Bhabhi ji. But remember, I am in the police department and have microscopic eyes so that no thief or adulterer escapes my eyes. If you fail, you have to abandon two days of making charges. Come to my house in the morning around ten."

Ghasi Ram reached Vipul's house in the morning with some professional tools, such as, an anvil, a tiny hammer, a pair of tongs, crucibles, wire-gauge and many other small things. After expressing sincerest apologies, Vipul's attendant searched him and his pockets for any piece of metal. Placing the gold coins into a crucible, Ghasi Ram created coal-fire around it, melted and shaped the coins into a little rod.

Meanwhile, a woman passed by in front of Vipul's house, shouting, "Take buttermilk, take buttermilk, very tasty."

Ghasi Ram requested Vipul to buy a glass of buttermilk from her and adding some black salt and ground *jeera* – cumin seeds, he drank it, saying, "I take it daily and feel refreshed by it."

For two days, Ghasi Ram worked very hard to make two gold bangles. In between, many tools were needed from his house and his assistant was sent to fetch them but each time both ways he was thoroughly searched. Of course, he was not allowed to join Ghasi Ram's working room.

On the third day, the bangles were nearly ready except for some last minute touches. As the buttermilk-selling lady came, Ghasi Ram, as usual, demanded a glass of it and drank it after adding black salt and *jeera* powder. Then he asked the lady, "Vimala, do you still have some buttermilk left in the pitcher? If so, how much would you charge for the remaining one?"

When she had said five rupees, Ghasi Ram requested Vipul to pay her five rupees as he would like to wash the new bangles thoroughly in the half-filled pitcher of buttermilk itself.

The lady agreed and gave the pitcher to Ghasi Ram who washed the bangles in the pitcher, rubbing them thoroughly, dipping them again and again till they shone perfectly.

After the lady had gone, he demanded a piece of clean cloth with which he rubbed the bangles forcefully till they shone like the new gold from mint. Wrapping them in a piece of thin pink paper, he placed them into a beautiful casket and gave it to Vipul, saying, "I could do no pilfering because of your and your attendant's microscopic eyes. The bangles are quite pure. You can go and have them examined by any goldsmith."

Taking the casket, Vipul went to a goldsmith and asked him to ascertain how much gold and how much alloy the bangles contained.

The goldsmith rubbed them against the touchstone a couple of times and told him, "Vipul ji, they are all pure…"

"Pure gold."

"No, pure brass."

Failing to believe yet with a sense of shock, Vipul went to the second goldsmith who simply confirmed the findings of the first one.

Feeling convinced, Vipul went back to Ghasi Ram's house and said, "My friend I salute you. The gold bangles are all Kalpana's because you have earned them. These bangles are made of pure brass. It is difficult to believe that you could deceive so well the microscopic eyes of a police officer and his attendant. Now at least tell me how could you have transformed the gold bangles into brass ones?"

Folding his hands and touching Vipul's knees, Ghasi Ram explained, "Kindly forgive me, Vipul, I did it to meet your challenge. First of all, I was puzzled not knowing how to do it but my wife suggested a way out. As I prepared the gold bangles in your house, I prepared brass ones exactly of the same design and size at home in the night. On the third day, my wife kept the brass ones into the hawking lady's pitcher full of buttermilk. As I washed the gold bangles in the pitcher, I replaced them with the brass ones."

❖❖❖

19

THE HOLY COW

The youngest son is usually a holy cow for his parents. Since no child is expected to be born after him, he gets a lion's share of love and affection not only from parents but also from his elder brothers and sisters. Nanak Chand had eight children – seven sons and one daughter and Hemant was the youngest of them. It was a time when having more and more children was considered an evidence of man's virility. In Danpur village of Lalitpur district in U.P., Nanak was also considered blessed by god or else there are hundreds of couples who despite their pilgrimages, prayers and offerings to gods and goddesses for children remain disappointed in the absence of any child.

A large family has its own pleasures. There is an atmosphere of perpetual festivity at home. All the children played different games. During the extreme winter, all the children slept on the bed of brown straws by spreading them out on the bare earth and then covering it with a bed-spread. On looking back after many years, Roop Kishore, found that the bed made of bare-straws was more comfortable than the rubberized mattress people use today. Before a thick sheet of cloth was spread on, it formed a good arena for jumping and mischief-making. The siblings threw handfuls of straws at one another as children play with snow-balls in cold countries. High-jumps, long jumps and somersaults were tried on it without hurting anyone since the spread out straws were nearly one-foot thick.

When Hemant grew up a little and began to take solids, Roop Kishore, his eldest brother, would place him in his lap and feed him. Though he was married at that time, he loved him as his son. Roop Kishore worked as Lecturer in Physics in Government College, Gwalior. When he took his wife Chandravati with him, Hemant was a three-year old child. He was sent to Gwalior to accompany his eldest brother Roop Kishore so that his newly married Bhabhi would not have to remain alone in her first ever visit to a new place immediately after marriage.

Both Roop Kishore and his wife Chandravati loved Hemant as their own son. Whenever he went out of station to participate in a conference or to conduct practical examinations in any city, he made it a point to bring all sorts of toys for Hemant who felt very happy and showed them to others with a sense of pride. Even when Roop Kishore's first son was born, Hemant would continue to sleep with his brother and would wet the bed in which the latter would remain for the whole night so that the child might not catch cold.

In the morning, when Roop Kishore would tease Hemant, "You wetted the bed in the night. You are a dirty child."

"No. I am not. You are a dirty child. You might have done it yourself. " Turning to Chandravati, Hemant asked, "Bhabhi ji, do you think I could have wetted the bed? Am I a dirty child?"

Picking him up in her hands and kissing him, Chandravati said, "No, you could not have done it. Your Bhaisahib could have done it."

Sometimes Roop Kishore and his wife had to give in to the whimsical and unreasonable demands of Hemant. Once Chandravati arranged during Navaratra time, a *kanya-bhoj* – feast for girls, in which she distributed frocks to each one of them. Seeing the other girls with frocks, Hemant demanded that he too be given a girl's frock! Both Roop Kishore and Chandravati attempted to convince him that he was a boy, that he should have a male dress but obstinate as Hemant was, he refused to yield. Finally, they let him wear a girl's frock.

Happily in the frock, Hemant went out in the neighbourhood where everyone made fun of him. One boy said, "Hema Rani, you are a beautiful girl. When are you going to your husband?"

"I am not a girl; I am a boy," he said.

"No, you are a girl. You wear a frock"

Others too teased him that he was a girl and not a boy. Troubled by the taunts, Hemant went back home, took off the frock and put his own shirt on.

By the time, Hemant was seven-year old. Roop Kishore had his own two sons – Neelesh and Anikesh – four and two-year olds respectively. It was at such a time that Roop Kishore's father told him to continue keeping Hemant with him so that he could have a good education in the city, particularly under his supervision as he was a college Lecturer.

Danpur village had only a Government High School in which most children of the village studied. All Roop Kishore's younger brothers and sister also studied in it. Since Hemant was Nanak's favourite son – a holy cow – he wanted him to get the best education which was possible only in the city. Roop Kishore explained it was true that the education in the city was very good but it was quite expensive and he would not be able to shoulder the burden of Hemant's education when he had his own two sons. When Roop Kishore pointed out this fact to his father, the latter asked him in a rough tone, "Can't you do this for me?"

Roop Kishore got Hemant admitted to a Convent school in which his fees was three times more than the combined fees of his own two sons. While there was no tutor for his own sons, Roop Kishore had to engage a tutor for Hemant. His elder son Neelesh complained about this discrimination, "Father, why am I not admitted to convent school as Hemant is?"

Roop Kishore told him a lie, "His father gives me money for him but for you everything has to go from my pocket and my salary does not allow it."

On the last day of the month, Roop Kishore, his wife and both their sons invariably sat together to prepare the next month's budget. Roop used to take their proposals – clothes, shoes and other household items informally during the course of the month but finalise the budget for the next month on the last day so that they could manage the monthly expenses well. The budget proposals often went twice as much as his salary was. When he would point out this fact to others, his one son would request him, "Please cut down my shoes. I'll get the old ones mended."

The other son would say, "Cut down my shirt, I can manage with the old one."

Chandravati was the most hard-working member in the house and it would have been quite difficult for her husband to cut down her saree. Knowing her husband's feelings, she crossed out the saree herself.

On the other hand, there was no cut as far as Hemant's expenses were concerned. Though his father sent merely some grains and lentils, Roop Kishore had to spend all the expenses incurred in Hemant's education. Normally, he would have spent it with pleasure because Hemant was his youngest brother, but the problem was that Hemant's way of living drew a comparison with his own sons and began to breed in them an inferiority complex. Once his elder son said, "Papa, all the students think that all three of us are brothers. Then they ask us why our clothes are so cheap whereas Hemant puts on very good ones."

The youngest son Anikesh said, "There was a little tear in the collar of my shirt. Hemant put his finger into it, and made the tear wider and then made fun of me before other neighbouring children that the collar has been nibbled by me."

Both the children did not say anything directly to their father; they told their mother about it. Roop Kishore wanted them to learn a lesson in simple living but the way Hemant was showing off, it was becoming counter-productive.

It pained Roop Kishore many times that his own children should suffer from inferiority complex and live in forced simplicity because of paucity of funds whereas he himself occupied such a prestigious post.

It was winter time and the children used to go to their schools in woolen pants and coats. Learning the lesson in economy well, Neelesh had taken a shirt from Hemant who was going to throw because of its frayed cuffs. Neelesh had made it sleeveless by chopping off its sleeves. He felt that since no one knows what kind of sleeves one has under the woolen coat, he made use of the sleeveless shirt during the time of urgency. Hemant, going to the convent school, of course, had altogether new clothes, refusing to wear those which had developed some tears in them. For a number of weeks, there was no problem. One day a medical team visited the Government High School for medical checkup of students. They were asked to remove their coats which Neelesh gently declined. When the Principal became angry, he had to remove his coat. The students and teachers then found out that he had a sleeveless shirt under his coat. There was a spontaneous uproar of laughter. Neelesh wished the earth had opened up and swallowed him into it.

When he came home, he wept bitterly. In between his ceaseless hiccups, he narrated the entire story. The worse part came later when Hemant and other children, hearing of the story from their neighbouring friends, made fun of Neelesh.

One friend of Hemant said loudly within the hearing of Neelesh, "Till now I had heard of sleeveless blouses but now some boys have started a new fashion of wearing sleeveless shirts."

"It's decidedly a new fashion," another friend of Hemant said.

"But why did you put it on?" Neelesh's friend asked him. "You have other good shirts."

"Other shirts were not ironed," Neelesh said. "I had one ironed shirt which I was going to wear but Hemant had borrowed my ironed shirt and requested me to put on the sleeveless shirt. First of all, I declined but my mother said that Hemant was my uncle and hence I should agree to it."

Neelesh's friend said, "And he is the one who is spreading this news among friends of yours and making fun of you."

"That's what troubles me," Neelesh said.

"Don't feel upset," Roop Kishore consoled. "Such things are forgotten with the passage of time."

"What I mind is that it was my shirt that Hemant had taken and rather than being quiet, he has been laughing vigorously, taunting me with his friends since the moment he got information from other neighboring children."

Whenever anything new came in the house, the first preference was given to Hemant. Being Roop Kishore's youngest brother, he was the eldest among the three children in the house and hence Neelesh and Anikesh had to show proper respect to him. The question the two sons often raised with their mother was whether the person deserved that respect! To them, Hemant appeared to be an intruder. Neelesh and his younger brother felt that their rights were being encroached upon by his uncle.

One day feeling sore over the forced respect that he had to show to Hemant, Neelesh said in anger, "If he is my uncle, why doesn't he stay with his father as I stay with mine?"

Roop Kishore heard it with a sense of shock and said in a somewhat soft tone: "Hemant is my youngest brother. He is my father's holy cow. You should not say such things about him."

Once when his father was not there, Neelesh softly discussed the issue with his mother: "Mother, why does Hemant get so much money that he lives like a prince whereas we stay as paupers?"

She placed her loving hand on his head and said, "I understand your feelings my boy! Your grandfather had given good education to your father. Suppose for a moment, if he were not given the education, your father would have remained in the village ploughing the field or doing other menial jobs as your other uncles are doing in Danpur village."

While Neelesh and Anikesh planned to continue their studies in Gwalior even after 12th standard, Hemant insisted on his father that he would like to go for Bachelor of Engineering degree in Maulana Azad College of Technology in Bhopal. Nanak Chand called Roop Kishore and insisted that he must send money every month to Hemant for five years of his studies and that he would pay it back after he takes up a job. I give you the guarantee."

It was a difficult proposition for Roop Kishore when both of his sons were ready to take education in Government Engineering College, Gwalior after a couple of years. When Roop expressed his difficulties before his father, the latter said, "You have to do this, Roop Kishore. I gave you complete education upto M.Sc. Now it is your responsibility to give complete education to your youngest brother. I have taken a promise from Hemant that he would pay your money back once he takes up a job. If not, I may sell a part of my land but I'll pay you all the expenses."

"Father," Roop Kishore humbly pleaded. "I do not have so much money. I'll have to take loan from my Provident Fund."

"That is your concern how you do it," Nanak Chand emphatically said. "But you have to do it; this is my order."

Roop Kishore had to agree to do it reluctantly. He knew that his father was a hard-task master and could take punitive steps by disinheriting him from the landed property.

For five long years, Roop Kishore continued to send monthly money orders to Hemant for his education in Bhopal. But during this period, he had to bear a lot of hardships. At one stage, he had to mortgage Chandravati's ornaments. The only consolation was that once Hemant gets a job, he would pay back all the money. When it is done, Roop Kishore will be able to clear his debt and get wife's ornaments back. After five years were over, it was a big relief for the entire family, including his children.

Luckily Hemant got a good job of an Engineer in Gwalior itself and began to live with Roop Kishore's family. Roop Kishore reminded him that as per his promises, he should return the money as his own children had grown up and were studying in an Engineering college in Gwalior. Hemant promised to do something about it and said, "I have seen the newly constructed flats and they are good. I'll pay for one of them which I will gift to you for all the help you had given me since my childhood. You wouldn't have to live in a rented accommodation."

However, Neelesh continued to express doubts about it to his father. Nevertheless, Roop Kishore had complete faith in Hemant and his promise made him happy that his sacrifices were being rewarded now.

When the flat was ready and registration done in Hemant's name, Roop Kishore asked him, "When are you going to transfer it into my name?"

"Why should I?" Hemant asked Roop Kishore in a harsh tone. "It has been purchased with my hard earnings."

Roop Kishore ironically asked, "Was my earning spent on your education without hard labour?"

"That is your concern," Hemant retorted. "The amount you sent to me was a part of your duty. As our father spent money for your education, you did it for me. The matter ends! I am shifting in the flat tomorrow."

Roop Kishore approached his father, reminding him of his promise that in case of Hemant's failure to pay back money, he himself would pay him but his response was no different from that of Hemant. Completely shocked and heart-broken, Roop Kishsore in a flash went over all the care and concern he and his wife had bestowed on Hemant and no less the hardships the entire family had to suffer for his education. In utter frustration and with tears in his eyes, Roop Kishore told the wholc shocking story to his wife and children, exclaiming in exasperation, "I have been cheated by a person whom I and my wife treated since his childhood better than our own sons!"

While Chandravati wiped off her tears, Neelesh said, "You used to call him your father's holy cow. Now you know how holy he is!"

❖❖❖

20

AMNESIA

The oft-quoted saying goes: "Old is gold" but in these days of adulteration, one does not specify its value in carats. Even dishonesty is not pure. Manav remembered a milkman telling his son: "Always tell truth, son."

"Father," the son said. "When I go to distribute milk to the customers, they often ask me whether I had mixed water in it? Should I say yes?"

"No," the father said, "because we don't put water into milk but put milk into water."

Manav was seventy five years old and had retired ten years back from the government service. He was the Principal of the Government Higher Secondary School, Satna in Madhya Pradesh. As long as he was in job, he was surrounded by the teachers, clerks and students who flattered him in every possible way whether what they said to him was true or not. But their comments made him very happy because he failed to scrutinise how much alloy their golden talks contained.

The reality came to his understanding only after his retirement from the government job, when he had no administrative power in hand. Those very teachers who never left him alone and praised his shining bald pate, his well-ironed clothes, his sense of accommodation of teachers, his manners and courtesies, even his shabbily polished shoes now turned their faces away on sighting him advancing towards them as if he were suffering from Corona or some other infectious disease. There was time when he received dozens of "Good Morning" messages on his WhatsApp account; now it became silent as if the flies hovering and buzzing over the sweet porridge were gone.

Since Manav got a good amount of money as pension from the Government of Madhya Pradesh, he had no problem as far as finances were concerned. During his tenure as the Principal, he had got a good house constructed in Satna. His son and daughter were already married and lived happily in New Delhi. What weighed heavily on Manav was a growing sense of estrangement and loneliness from his one-time colleagues, his friends and even his children. It is this sense of alienation which made him brooding all the time and that increased his blood-pressure while affecting his memory.

Many times to get rid of his boredom and to keep his mind free from tension, he would sit with his mobile phone, flip through the YouTube or Facebook posts, look at political or culinary arts, or about the foretelling stars but after sometime they too appeared boring and he turned the instrument off.

Sometimes it appeared to him that his head was becoming hot. Manav read the local newspaper, every column, every news item including matrimonial advertisements and obituary notices. But after sometime, it too bored him. One of his well-wishers suggested that he better do some writing work which keeps a person occupied, saves him from boredom and improves his memory. Manav did not know how to write poems, essays or stories and hence did not know what to write. The friend suggested that the Gayatri temple gives some blank notebooks on which a devotee has to write Gayatri *mantra* all over till the notebook is completely filled up and then return it to the temple and get a new one. Manav brought a notebook and wrote the Gayatri *mantras* on a large number of pages and felt a little happy by this act. Feeling very cheerful and victorious, Manav came to the kitchen for a glass of water. Seing him cheerful, Vanita complimented him, "So you have become a writer! Congratulations!"

Taken aback because Manav had not disclosed anything to her, he asked her, "How do you know it? I never told you."

Vanita giggled and said, "Do you remember you had told me once that your class fellows in the primary school used to tell you what you had eaten by your tell-tale shirt showing some grains of rice and *daal* on it. Now a palm-width of blue ink spot under the pocket of your shirt shows that you have begun to write."

Manav looked at the shirt and realised that in his forgetfulness he had kept the ink-pen in his pocket with its cap on the wrong side. Consequently, the pen had leaked and its ink had seeped down the pocket to create a patch of blue cloud on his shirt.

Frustrated with the writing work, Manav threw the notebook aside. Nothing seemed to give him pleasure, or even relief from the life of boredom. He felt his wife was lucky because she remained busy in the kitchen always doing something or the other though her memory too was getting affected. He never felt bored as long as he was in the job; his boredom slowly crept upon him after his retirement from job and near-desertion of him by his erstwhile colleagues and acquaintances.

Manav's inactivity, boredom, tension and the gradual dragging of time were constantly slowing down his mind. Sometimes the names of people and places he had met or seen hundreds of times disappeared from his mind. The forgotten name would attempt to knock at his mind's door, give its vague form whether it was one, two or three-syllabled word but refused to come in recognisable totality. Manav ransacked his head many times, scratched it with his finger nails but nothing happened. He attempted to associate the names with something or the other so that he could recall them through association of ideas. To remember his old friend Doorwar, he associated the name with the door, tied Phool Chand's name with a fool, Ram Niwas's with Ayodhya which is Ram's residence but such a thing did not always succeed in clicking his head with the right name. It was a kind of proof that something or the other was adversely affecting his memory.

Though his wife Vanita also had the same problem, it was not in the same intensity. While taking care of the house, she would place some item at one place and would go on searching everywhere for it. The mobile phones of both Manav and Vanita often played hide-and-seek game with them. Whenever she misplaced it, Manav would use his mobile phone to dial her number and she would do the same when he happened to misplace his. There were times, rare ones, when both of them happened to misplace their mobile phones and at such times, the landline phone would come to their rescue.

One day Manav did not remember his wife's name. Sometimes, half-jocularly, instead of calling her by her name, he would address her at home as, "Pappoo's mother" or "Do you hear?" or "Bhagyawan" – the lucky one, but in front of visitors or outsiders, he always called her by her real name. Now suddenly when his friend came to spend a few minutes with him for gossiping and for exchanging political news, Manav called his wife, "Darling, please come here for a minute."

After he had told her to prepare two cups of tea and she had gone back, Manav's friend asked him, "For how long have you been married?"

After some calculation, Manav said, "Fifty years."

"And you still call your wife darling!"

He quietly put his mouth to his friend's ear and whispered, "Because just now I forgot her name. Sometimes some names are temporarily blocked out of my memory."

Some people attributed his transitory blockage of memory to acidity whereas others to his growing age. Whatever the reason, it was quite irritating and sometimes equally amusing. He laughed when his wife forgot and she laughed when he did. Consequently, they provided short giggles to each other.

Many times, Vanita would go to the refrigerator, open it but would remain standing before it, not remembering why she had reached there. Then she would go back to the kitchen and remember that she had gone to take out a lemon or a tomato. Similar things happened with Manav. He would come down the staircase and stand there staring, not remembering whether he had come down the staircase or was to go up.

Even though Manav's reflexes had slowed down, once in a while he drove his white Maruti car for short distances. Since he was to receive a relation coming from Rewa and since the Satna railway station was quite close to his residence, he drove his car and parked it very close to an electric pole so that he would not forget its parking place, as he often did in the past. After his relation had come, Manav attempted to unlock his car but found that the key was not getting inside the keyhole. For a moment, he suspected that some car thief might have fiddled with the lock with a duplicate key to steal it but it might not have worked. He felt lucky that his car was still there. Meanwhile, a man approached him with a policeman and the latter asked, "Are you stealing this gentleman's car?"

"No. This car is mine," Manav confidently said.

They asked his car number and after he had given it to them, they pointed out to the car parked next to the one he was claiming to be his. Feeling embarrassed, Manav went to the next car, checked its number, and drove it back home.

One day both Manav and Vanita were to go to Rewa by train. They normally made lists of items to be taken a couple of days in advance so that at the last minute they might not forget anything. An hour or so before leaving their house, they checked everything and were all ready to go. Once more the list was taken. Manav read it out aloud and Vanita nodded her head to say that everything was kept.

It was getting dark and they were all ready to leave. Before locking the main door of the house, Vanita picked up her purse and kept it pressed under her left arm. As she was about to make a move, she realised that one of her chappals was missing. She frantically searched for it everywhere. Manav looked for it but could not find. Meanwhile he did not remember where he had kept the new pair of his eye glasses and began to look for it everywhere.

"What are you looking for in the pockets of your shirts?" Vanita asked in anger. "My chappal can't be there?"

"I am looking for my spectacles" Manav said. "Please search for my spectacles. You can use another pair of chappals but I would go blind without my eyeglasses."

As Vanita was searching for her missing piece of chappals in the shoe-rack, Manav told her, "My eye glasses can't be there on the shoe-rack."

"You know well Manav that I am looking for one of my chappals."

Both of them went on searching for their respective items frantically because they could not have gone without them. So much engrossed were they in their searches that they had no time to look at each other. Since the time was approaching fast to catch the train, they were sweating and gasping, running around here and there, recollecting the places where they might have kept their respective items. In any case, they did not want to miss the train. Vanita meanwhile brought Manav's old pair of eyeglasses and said, "Use this piece in place of the new one, otherwise we would miss the train."

As Vanita began to put the old pair of spectacles over his eyes, she found that the new pair of eyeglasses was already on Manav's eyes which neither he nor she had noticed earlier. She said, "You are such a sweet forgetful husband. You don't even remember that you already have your new pair of glasses on your eyes!"

It was a matter of relief that at least one of the two items was found. As Vanita had stretched her hands to put the new glasses on his eyes, something had fallen down from under her left arm. Manav looked at the fallen item and was surprised to find that it was her missing chappal, not the purse, which she was supposed to be holding in her armpit. Picking up the fallen piece of chappals, Manav gave it to her, saying, "This is your missing chappal. You were having it under your armpit and thinking it was your purse."

"My purse has the same kind of strap as my chappals and I had incidentally kept it on the shoe-rack," Vanita weakly attempted to justify her mistake.

With smiles on their faces, they looked at each other and locked the door. Manav said, "You are a great forgetful wife. Together, we make a wonderful forgetful couple."

❖❖❖